GW00976179

AFTER TRAGEDY
Three Irish plays
THE GIGLI CONCERT
BAILEGANGAIRE
CONVERSATIONS ON A HOMECOMING

'Thomas Murphy has always taken risks, the risk of delving into the human psyche, the risk of putting fierce emotions to work on stage, the risk of trying to transcend the ordinary. In **The Gigli Concert** he stakes everything.'

Fintan O'Toole, *Sunday Tribune*

'The point where fact and fantasy meet, as so often is the case in rural Ireland, is indistinguishably emmeshed in mythology, hypocrisy and repression – and it is the unwinding of this hurting, hateful spool that lends **Bailegangaire** its compulsive narrative delights. All is expressed in a staggeringly poetic Anglo-Irish idiom which gives fleeting glimpses, when mists clear, of a world away, away beyond the dull grasp of the Anglicised here and now.'

Sheila Fox, *City Limits*

THOMAS MURPHY was born in Tuam, Co. Galway. In 1962 he retired from teaching to become a full-time writer in London. He returned to Ireland in 1970. He was a member of the Board of Directors of the Abbey Theatre from 1972–1983, and was Writer in Association with the Druid Theatre Company, Galway, from 1983–1985. He currently holds the position of Writer in Association with the Abbey Theatre. He has written plays for the BBC, RTE and Thames television and he has directed plays in Ireland and New York. His work includes **A Crucial Week in the Life of a Grocer's Assistant** (BBC TV, 1967, Abbey Theatre, Dublin 1969), **Famine** (Peacock Theatre, Dublin, 1968 and two performances Royal Court, London, 1969), **The Sanctuary Lamp** (Abbey Theatre, Dublin, 1976), **A Whistle in the Dark** (Theatre Royal Stratford East, 1961, Long Wharf Theatre, New Haven, Connecticut & New York), **The Gigli Concert** (Abbey Theatre, Dublin, 1983) winner of the Harvey's Best Play Award and the Independent Newspapers Theatre Award; **Bailegangaire** (Druid Theatre Company, Galway, 1985, Donmar Warehouse, London, 1986, BBC Radio, 1987) winner of the Harvey's Best Play Award 1985–1986 and the Sunday Tribune Theatre Award 1985–1986 which was also awarded for **Conversations on a Homecoming** (Druid Theatre Company, Galway, 1985, Donmar Warehouse, London, 1987). Thomas Murphy is a member of Aosdána and the Irish Academy of Letters. He lives in Dublin.

The photograph on the front cover shows a detail from 'Reflection with two children (self portrait)', 1965. Oil on canvas, 36 x 36 inches, by Lucian Frend. Thyssen – Bornemisza Collection, Lugano, Switzerland.

By the same author

Published by the Gallery Press:

ON THE OUTSIDE
  (*in collaboration with Noel O'Donoghue*)
A WHISTLE IN THE DARK
A CRUCIAL WEEK IN THE LIFE OF A GROCER'S ASSISTANT
THE ORPHANS
FAMINE
THE MORNING AFTER OPTIMISM
THE WHITE HOUSE
ON THE INSIDE
THE VICAR OF WAKEFIELD (*Adaptation*)
SHE STOOPS TO CONQUER (*Adaptation*)
THE SANCTUARY LAMP
THE J. ARTHUR MAGINNIS STORY
THE BLUE MACUSHLA
THE INFORMER (*Adaptation*)
A THIEF OF A CHRISTMAS

AFTER TRAGEDY

Three Irish plays by
THOMAS MURPHY

With a preface by
Christopher Murray

THE GIGLI CONCERT
BAILEGANGAIRE
CONVERSATIONS
ON A HOMECOMING

A METHUEN PAPERBACK

A METHUEN NEW THEATRESCRIPT

This collection first published in Great Britain as a paperback original in 1988 by Methuen London Ltd., 11 New Fetter Lane, London EC4P 4EE and in the United States of America by Methuen Inc., 29 West 35th Street, New York, NY 10001

The Gigli Concert first published in 1984 by The Gallery Press
and reprinted here in a revised version.
Copyright © Thomas Murphy 1984, 1988

Bailegangaire first published in 1986 by The Gallery Press
and reprinted here in a revised version.
Copyright © Thomas Murphy 1986, 1988

Conversations on a Homecoming first published in 1986 by The Gallery Press
and reprinted here in a revised version.
Copyright © Thomas Murphy 1986, 1988

Preface copyright © 1988 Methuen London Ltd
This collection copyright © Thomas Murphy 1988

British Library Cataloguing in Publication Data

Murphy, Thomas, *1935–*
    After tragedy : three Irish plays
    1. Drama in English, 1945– Texts
    I. Title
    822'.914

    ISBN 0–413–18600–8

Printed and bound in Great Britain by Richard Clay Ltd Bungay, Suffolk

CAUTION
All performing rights in these plays are strictly reserved. Applications should be made in advance to Fraser & Dunlop Ltd., 91 Regent Street, London W1R 8RU or Ms B. Aschenbuerg, ICM, 40 West 57th Street, New York, NY 10019.

This paperback is sold subject to the condition that it shall not, by way of trade or otherwise, be lent, resold, hired out, or otherwise circulated without the publisher's prior consent in any form of binding or cover other than that in which it is published and without a similar condition including this condition being imposed on the subsequent purchaser.

CONTENTS

PREFACE

Whatever the reason, Tom Murphy (b. 1935) doesn't seem to have the high profile he deserves. Among the most daring and challenging of his generation, his drama not only commands admiration but cries out for greater world attention than it has enjoyed.

Following the success of his first full-length play, *A Whistle in the Dark* (1961), which had its première at the Theatre Royal, Stratford East, Murphy mainly made his career in Ireland, becoming a member of the Abbey Theatre's Board of Directors and consolidating his reputation as an adventurous, hard-hitting and unpredictable writer. *Famine* (1968), a powerful, rough-textured play exploring the moral collapse of a community (just as *A Whistle in the Dark* explores the moral collapse of an individual), showed its strength as epic drama when revived by the Druid Theatre Company in 1984. *The Morning after Optimism* (1971), in which the late Colin Blakely gave a memorable performance, scrutinized the feelings of middle age by means of a fantastic encounter in a forest with a youthful, idealistic alter ego. Violence is never far from the surface of a Murphy play, and the ending of *The Morning after Optimism* recalls the primal, fratricidal duel of *A Whistle in the Dark:* 'Now I know who you are,' says the young Edmund, as he embraces his long-lost brother; 'Now you can be sure of it,' replies James, as he stabs him in the back. The moment of betrayal is the moment of truth. *The Sanctuary Lamp* (1975) was another search play, as one ex-circus performer pursues another in order to settle a score; he finds him inside a Catholic church, employed as sacristan. In this setting the friends battle it out through the night, drinking altar wine and raking over their beliefs. The play upset a lot of people during its Abbey première, because of its iconoclasm, but its sheer verbal energy (of the kind John Osborne used to have and lost after *A Sense of Detachment*) stamps it as one of Murphy's finest achievements.

In the later 1970s Murphy seemed to lose his way. He gave up writing for the stage and took up gardening. A flop with *The Blue Macushla* (1980) had many Dublin heads shaking while intoning Patrick Kavanagh's line, 'He's finished and that's definitely.' Then came *The Gigli Concert* (1983) and Murphy's work entered an exciting new phase.

The Gigli Concert is a big play, three hours long, uncompromising in its demands on audience endurance, yet carrying such an impact in performance that (although it didn't finish until 11.30 p.m.) its première got a standing ovation at the Abbey Theatre. The play tells of an Irish millionaire who is undergoing a mental breakdown. Like Ibsen's Master Builder, he has built a thousand homes and suddenly finds that he doesn't want to build any more: 'This – something – cloud has come down on me.' The form his depression takes is a crazy longing to sing like Gigli, and he goes for help not to a psychiatrist but to a quack calling himself a dynamatologist, a hopeless wreck whom we first encounter greeting the world with the cry, 'Christ, how am I going to get through today?' In taking on the assignment, the quack JPW King ('I have the letters before my name') finds himself in intimate relation to a sick soul. There is an extraordinary moment in Scene Five when the Man breaks down in *'Terrible dry sobbing . . . as if from the bowels of the earth.'* The horror of what he has done with his life strikes home, and we begin to see the Faustian shape of the play. The obsession with Gigli's voice ('He's the devil!') transfers to King at the point when the Man's bad faith asserts itself: once again, the moment of (self) betrayal is the moment of truth. The Man draws back from seeing himself; instead, he heals himself by readjusting to the world that is destroying him. King, pathetic and alienated as he is, takes up the challenge that it is possible to work magic like Faustus and to sing like Gigli. Crazed, drunken, hammered by awareness of loss and failure, King finally makes the magic happen on stage, as he sings like Gigli. Theatrically daring, this ending marks a new spirit of transcendence in Murphy's work.

In spring 1985, the Druid Theatre, Galway, where Murphy was Writer-in-Association for a year, premièred *Conversations on a Homecoming*. This re-write of an earlier work (*The White House,* Abbey Theatre, 1972) has since been seen in upstate New York, in Sydney, and in London, lifting Murphy's career into long-denied prominence abroad. Set in a public house in the west of Ireland in the early 1970s the play exposes the disillusion of a community betrayed by its belief in a hero, JJ, who once had raised all local hopes through his identification with John F. Kennedy. Like Behan's Quare Fellow, JJ does not appear on stage, but his drunken, demoralized presence haunts it nevertheless, as several friends gather in his public house to welcome home his disciple, Michael, from America. Michael, romantic idealist and failed actor, is unmasked in the course of an evening's carousing that builds in cruelty and fun-and-games of the kind Albee used so devastatingly in *Who's Afraid of Virginia Woolf?* Murphy's main truth-teller is Tom, a teacher with a whiplash tongue and a nice eye for pretenders. Liam, former medical student turned auctioneer, well on his way to becoming the Man in *The Gigli Concert*, is pin-pointed in Tom's dismissal: 'You're only a fuckin' bunch of keys!' Liam is a symptom of a society that has lost its way and believes in cynical opportunism and ersatz American notions of beauty, art and success.

The country itself, Tom charges, is too ready to 'follow to the death any old bollocks with a borrowed image, any old JJ who has read a book on American politics or business methods. Jesus, images: fuckin' neon shadows.' Jimmy Porter, in his prime could hardly have put it better. But Murphy is not just sounding off. The play is, indeed, stark naturalism up to a point, and the authenticity certainly depends on the strong kidneys of the actors as they get through a vast amount of Guinness on their way towards putting several records straight. But before the end there is a characteristic scene, which suddenly lifts the action beyond naturalism. In a moment of quiet, Peggy sings the song – JJ's song – redolent of the old days when hope was alive for these people. It is 'All in the April evening,' by Katharine Tynan. Since the lambs remind the poet of the Lamb of God the poem becomes a discovery of God in the midst of pain:

> The lambs were weary, and crying
> With a weak, human cry.
> I thought on the Lamb of God
> Going meekly to die.

Into a dark world of disillusion on stage comes this beautiful note of faith and understanding, opening up behind the sordid picture of provincial life another horizon, a perspective of a redeemed world. Music is vital to a Murphy play. Indeed, his plays aspire, as Walter Pater said of all art, to the condition of music, a notion that may seem less pretentious than it sounds if one recalls the line in *The Gigli Concert*: 'Singing [is] . . . the only possible way to tell people . . . who you are.' In that sense, perhaps, the audience is the music while the music lasts.

In the same year as *Conversations* was premièred, the Druid Company also staged Murphy's *Bailegangaire* (pron. *balya-gon-gawra*, 'The Town-without-laughter'). With the late Siobhán McKenna in the role of Mommo it proved a shattering and heart-warming play about three women bound together by the past. Sometimes commentators regard this play as related to or even deriving from Beckett's *Happy Days*, but in fact Murphy could readily identify with Sean O'Casey's comment, 'I have nothing to do with Beckett. He isn't in me; nor am I in him.' *Happy Days* is a surrealist play, a witty symbolist's depiction of what it means, literally, to come down in the world and to be stuck in a rut. Murphy's forte is naturalism. His characters always have a history and a controlling environment. He presents life not as absurd or a mistake but as ultimately worthwhile and beautiful. His Mommo never despairs, and she succeeds at last in creating order out of the mess of history, and thereby she frees herself and her two granddaughters from its grip. She who quotes her father's words of wisdom lives to offer a gloss on them by her courage and humanity: 'in the wondrous handiwork of God, [I] have found only two flaws, man an' the earwig. Of what use is man, what utility the earwig, where do they either fit in the system? They are both specimens desperate, without any control and therefore unfree.' What is the use of a senile old woman of 'four score year and upward, not an hour more nor less?' The challenge of the play lies in its humanistic answer to such an un-Beckettian Lear-like question.

An interesting feature of *Bailegangaire* is its use of time. There are two levels: the present, in which Mary and Dolly, the two victims of the very tragedy with which Mommo is obsessed, struggle to come to terms with their lives; and the past, in which Mommo's consciousness is buried. At first these two worlds seem comically juxtaposed, with the ravings of the old woman in the bed only an intrusion on the concerns of the younger women. But it becomes clear that the clue to their lives and to their struggle for a sense of freedom and purpose lies in the old woman. The two time schemes begin to come together when Mary joins in the narrative in earnest, urging Mommo to finish the story of the fatal laughing contest, with its hubristic, tragic outcome. Action gives way to narrative; the word becomes all important, made, indeed, (charred) flesh as the truth is spoken at last. When this happens, Mary's frustrated present and Dolly's pregnant future suddenly merge with the past, with the recitation of 'misfortunes' that bind this family, this audience, this world together in the common name of humanity. It is a beautiful and cathartic moment when Mary and Dolly lie down with the old woman in the bed. Their histories are woven together in an image of love. Mommo gathers in her 'fondlings' around her, and like Maurya in *Riders to the Sea* says her prayers and accepts life as a vale of tears. It is thus Synge rather than Beckett one should think of when assessing the merits of *Bailegangaire*.

Mention of Synge, however, mustn't blind one to Murphy's searing contemporaneity. Murphy is significant because he articulates the feelings audiences have today of bafflement, frustration and anxiety in the face of crumbling certainties and bogus alternatives. He seems to speak for his time. His persisting theme is authenticity: how to live, to sustain identity, in conditions that conspire to corrupt or to destroy the self. The later plays, in particular, challenge us initially with images of bad faith and/or of evasion. But they leave us, in the end, with new images, minted from the human compulsion to be free: images of courage and of love.

Christopher Murray, 1987

THE GIGLI
CONCERT

The Gigli Concert was first performed at the Abbey Theatre, Dublin, on Thursday, 29 September 1983 with the following cast:

JPW KING	Tom Hickey
IRISH MAN	Godfrey Quigley
MONA	Kate Flynn

Directed by Patrick Mason
Designed by Bronwen Casson with
                         Frank Hallinan Flood
Lighting by Tony Wakefield

Set: JPW's office which is also his living quarters, in Dublin.

Note: the trio from *Attila* might be used as an 'overture' but Beniamino Gigli's voice singing 'O Paradiso' introduces the play and continues for some moments into Scene One; other arias – sung by Gigli – bridge the scenes and continue through the intermission.

The aria 'Tu che a Dio spiegasti l'ali' on page 34 is the 'Pearl' recording with Gigli, bass and chorus; the same aria on page 39 is a different 'Pearl' recording: Gigli, solo voice (without bass and chorus). Refer 'Pearl' Records.

The IRISH MAN's 'Ida' story, pages 49–50, is embraced by 'Toselli's Serenade.' In the trio from '*Atilla*' – 'Tu sol quest anima' – page 37 the opening soprano solo to be associated with MONA, the tenor solo with JPW's action, and the following bass solo to be associated and timed with the IRISH MAN's entrance.

Scene One

A table lamp with a red shade, switched on, and a shaft of yellow light from the washroom off. JPW's appearance complements his dingy surroundings (not yet clearly defined). He looks like a seedy private-eye. He is English, upper middle class, tempering his accent at times with an Irish intonation and some Irishisms . . .

He is seated at one end of his desk, scraping the remains of a pot of jam on to a piece of bread; washing down his breakfast with a careful measure from the remains of a bottle of vodka. He interrupts this business to make some illegal adjustment to the telephone connection-box on the wall, then his intense concentration rapping out a number on his telephone with the edge of his hand. (His rapping is illegal phone-tapping: all this a recurring action when he wants to use the phone) his vulnerability, waiting, holding his breath.

JPW: . . . Me . . . Fine . . . Is it? . . . Yes usually sunny after . . . Yes, and crisp . . . after frost . . . No, I'm still here. Same answer I suppose? (*Silently.*) Please . . . (*He nods solemnly to her reply.*) . . . 'Bye. What? . . . No, I shan't phone you again . . . I promise . . . I promise . . . 'Bye.

He goes to the window and lets up the blind. Morning light into the room defining the set. Faded lettering on the street-side of the window 'JPW KING – DYNAMATOLOGIST'. He stands looking out over the roofs of the city.

Christ, how am I going to get through today?

The office is dingy. A bed that converts into a couch, a desk with a telephone, a kettle, filing cabinet, clothes about the place, books, dusty charts on a wall and a photograph of 'Steve', another wall and door in frosted-glass panels, flowers withering in a vase, an old leather bag (suitcase) . . .

A ring of a bell on an outer door. A second and third ring. JPW becoming wary. Into action: re-adjustment to telephone connection-box. Outer door opening and the silhouette of a MAN in the next room, outside the frosted-glass panels. MAN knocking at door . . .

JPW: Yes? . . . Who is it?

MAN: Mr King?

JPW: Who is it? . . . Who is that?

MAN: Can I come in?

JPW: Pardon?

MAN: To talk.

JPW: What? . . . To what?

MAN (*muffled*): To sing.

JPW: What did you say? . . . What did he say? To what? . . . Hello? Hello? . . . Bloody hell.

Breakfast things into drawers, bed reconverted to couch, clothes stuffed away, too late to shave, but spectacles from somewhere for effect . . . he unlocks the glass-panelled door which leads to an anteroom.

Yes?

MAN: Mr King?

JPW: What?

MAN: Can I come in?

JPW: What do you want?

MAN: Ah . . . (*He comes in.*)

JPW: . . . There is possibly some mistake, Mr – Mr. (*Off, a church clock chiming the half hour.*) What time is it? Half-twelve?

MAN: Eleven.

JPW: I must get the lock on that (*outer*) door mended.

The MAN, though with head bowed, is talking in the dingy room. JPW assessing MAN: the expensive respectable dress, top coat, silk scarf, gloves, hat (hat a little out of keeping: '30s–40s American style – as worn by Gigli) and MAN's hand in his pocket, quietly toying with something – a recurring action – it could be a gun.

MAN: I . . .

JPW: Yes?

MAN: . . . happened to see your sign as I was passing.

JPW: What sign?

MAN: Are you the –? (*He nods at the lettering on the window.*)

JPW: Dynamatologist.

MAN: J.P.W. King.

JPW: I have the letters before my name.

MAN: You were letting up the blind.

JPW: Well, actually, I have been meaning to have that sign – removed?

MAN: I read something about you.

JPW: Me?

MAN: Your organisation.

JPW: Anything good?

MAN: Well, it was a few years ago. In the papers.

JPW: Personally, I thought that article a bit unfair myself. Hmm?

MAN *nods*.

I mean to say, water off my back as far as I am . . . you have not come about? (*the telephone*) Have you come to consult me?

MAN *considering* JPW.

I mean to say.

MAN: Yes.

JPW: Well, that's different. Yes, if you would care to? (*sit*) As you please. But lest there should be some misunderstanding I should say at the outset that dynamatology is not a military oriented movement. Self-realisation, you know? Because I had another caller, a gentleman of enquiring intellect, undoubtedly, yes, but had misinterpreted our meaning, in a trench-coat. Hmm? (MAN *nods*.) I knew that. As Steve puts it, mind is the essence of being alive. Steve, our founder and leader. Revolutionary thinker.

MAN: It said in the papers –

JPW: Water off my back: wanting us banned in Britain.

MAN: About ye saying anything is possible.

JPW: That is what I am explaining. The emphasis they put on the brain. But what is brain? Biological matter, meat. Mind is the essence. Yes?

MAN: I haven't much time for philosophy.

JPW: Busy man, aren't we all.

MAN: No. I've all the time in the world – if I want it.

JPW: Check. Your simple notion of life as substance is useful, I dare say, but we have gone beyond the macroscopic level into the subatomic world, and substance is simply – nonsense. Atoms, my friend. Atoms consist of whirlings – you may call them particles but we call them whirlings – and whirlings are not made of anything. But what are our whirlings presently doing? In layman's terms, dancing with each other, and that is an awful waste of energy. So what are we to do? Process of destratification until we arrive at that state we call Nihil where we can start putting our little dancers to proper work, and working properly they can go a very long way indeed to project you beyond the boundaries that are presently limiting you. Now you have a question.

MAN: How much?

JPW: Pardon?

MAN: Your fees.

JPW: Fees can wait. *The* priority, a good relationship of trust, mutual feed of energy between auditor – that's me – and subject. Okay?

MAN: I like to know where I stand.

JPW: Ten guineas a session – that's for six. But fifteen for the first in case it is going to be the only one. That was frankly put.

MAN: That's not too bad.

JPW: Do you think so?

MAN: It's fine.

JPW: Well, that was a good start. Well now, could we begin with your name?

MAN: Rather not.

JPW: That's good.

MAN: If you don't mind.

JPW: Your name! For God's sake, Mr–Mr, where has the orthodox route taken them? Into their very own not-very-pleasant strait-jackets. My style – as you have been observing – is casual.

MAN: I haven't much time for psychiatrists – psychologists.

JPW: Candid opinion? Intellectual philistines. Conflicting approaches, contradictory schools. And Freud! Now it transpires it was all about his having it off with his sister-in-law. Did you read about that? In the papers.

MAN: My wife wanted me to see a psychologist. Our doctor wanted me to see a psychiatrist. I told them the same thing.

JPW: What thing?

MAN: That I know more about life than the lot of them put together

JPW: I see. So you chose me?

MAN *considering* JPW.

Actually this stubble is going to be a beard.

MAN: You're a stranger here, Mr King?

JPW: Well, I have been here for nearly – five years? I mean to say.

MAN: But you're a stranger, you're English?

JPW: Yes, yes, but a Tipperary grandmother. That's where I get it from. God rest her.

MAN: Public school? (*Boarding school?*)

JPW: Yes.

MAN: I'm a self-made man.

JPW: I gathered that – I mean, and aren't you proud of it!

MAN: I should be.

JPW: And aren't you proud of it! I had my chances too.

MAN: But not university?

JPW: No, I broke my father's heart instead. But I got the trust money – eventually – (*Laughs again.*) And blew it! But that's enough about me, what do you think of me? Joke. Yes, well, time to start getting down to those old levels of data. We have no name, good. Address? No address, quite in order in my book. Telephone – in case? No. Fine. Age?

MAN: Fifty-one.

JPW: Ah! That rules out a few things, what? Yes, well. Are there many people of your acquaintance dying at the moment?

MAN (*rising*): I think . . .

JPW: We're doing fine.

MAN: I think we may have made a mistake.

They speak simultaneously:

JPW: Absolutely fine! –

MAN: I'll maybe call some other time –

JPW: You came to consult me –

MAN: No, I –

JPW: For my help –

MAN: I don't know what I'm doing here –

JPW: That's what I'm here for! Please –

Until:

MAN: I don't need help! (*Hand in his pocket.*) I've got the answer! Can't talk to anyone. I'm not insane!

JPW: I'm insane . . . I am insane. There, you nearly laughed.

MAN: I didn't.

JPW: I'm insane.

MAN: That's your problem.

JPW: I'm joking. That is what my father used to say, the boy is a dreamer, he used to say, he's crazy. Strike root was his phrase. Sit down, my friend. Mama, of course, was a different kettle of fish: the inner world, and a little poetry. What was your mother like?

MAN: Is it information you're looking for?

JPW: Or pace if you wish, yes, but, good heavens, if we cannot, two grown men, help one another. I mean to say do you think mental health means normal adjustment?

MAN: I don't want normal adjustment.

JPW: Exactly. Where is the achievement in standardised activity or routine trivia. Get out the old golf-clubs, take it out on a – a *ball?* Change your car, grow a carrot. I have to watch it myself, now that I have taken root. For God's sake, we might as well go back to Galileo Galilei, I say to my Helen.

MAN: I wouldn't call building more than a thousand houses routine trivia.

JPW: The house-proud life she would have me lead!

MAN: Apart from a thousand other deals.

JPW: So, you are a builder, a developer.

MAN: An 'operator'.

JPW: Got it. You have come to a standstill, you are looking for the will, the driveness to build a thousand more.

MAN: I don't want to build anything more. This – something – cloud has come down on me.

JPW: Has it happened before, is there a pattern?

MAN: I just felt I'd like an explanation.

JPW: Check. But no pattern?

MAN: I don't mind pain, I could always deal with pain. Could always – still can – and I've a bad back – mix concrete shovel for shovel with any navvy if a machine broke down. But this other thing. I don't understand it.

JPW: No pattern. Aything else?

MAN: What?

JPW: When you were outside the door I thought you said –

MAN: No, nothing else! How much did you say? (*Preparing to go.*)

JPW: You just want an explanation.

MAN: Ten, fifteen pounds? –

JPW: You stated it as a fact.

MAN: There's too many facts in the world. Them houses were built out of facts: corruption, brutality, back-handing, fronthanding, backstabbing, lump labour and a bit of technology.

JPW: I should not have thought you the type

MAN: Aaw, aren't yeh good? Oh, out there, boy, you learn how to take the main chance.

JPW: You don't have to pay me now. Your problem is –

MAN: Forget it. I have it here somewhere. Ten, eleven, fourteen . . .

JPW (*watching him make up the money with notes and coins*): . . . No, you forget it.

MAN: Fifteen. (*He sees JPW's offence; he laughs harshly, shortly.*) My problem is. Yeh, I didn't think you were such a funny man when I saw you standing in the window.

JPW: Your problem is not just a problem of life, life is the problem.

MAN: Out of a book? (*Puts money on desk.*) Fifteen pounds: fact.

JPW: Thank you. I owe you ten or fifteen minutes if you have no place else to go, and I do not think you have.

MAN: What would you like to talk about? You?

JPW: Anything you like.

MAN: . . . D'yeh like me hat? . . . I've come to a standstill. I was never a great one to talk much. Now I'd prefer to walk a mile in the other direction than say how yeh or fuck yeh to anyone. In the mornings I say Christ how am I going to get through today. The house is silent though there's a child in it. We were blessed with a late child. But I always managed to keep obscenities out of the house until lately. Now they're the only things that break the silence. Last week I was walking in the wood and my hat blew into the stream. No, not this one (*hat*).

JPW: You own a stream?

MAN: I kept trying to fish it out, but it kept on escaping so I started to shout. Obscenities. The wife come running. Her concern. Love, love, are you alright. Love. I don't want her concern. She's so – good. And I'm sure I hadn't opened my mouth to her in a month. I shouted. I'm entitled to my fucking moods. She was perplexed. Hah? I seen her age before my eyes. Then she walked away, like an old woman, through the trees. Beech. D'yeh know what a slashhook is?

JPW: Like a sickle.

MAN: Yeh. With a long shaft and more lethal. The following night I decided I'd deal with the itinerants. I'd took a couple of sleeping pills, some wine, but I knew I was in for another night with my music. (*Short, harsh laugh.*)

JPW: What pills?

MAN: Mandrax.

JPW: They've been taken off the market.

MAN (*dismisses this*): So, I decided I'd deal with the itinerants. The place is a shithouse. It's everywhere. Why did they choose me. Hmm? And I know the doorsteps where it belongs. The disrespect, to choose me, camp beside my territory, and the fuckers in this country. So. *Went* out. To kill them. But someone – the wife! – had called the police, and they stopped me. I would've killed them otherwise. No question 'bout that. Jail – hospital mean nothing to me. Jail – hospital have a certain appeal. Then I listened to the record for the rest of the night.

JPW: The police?

MAN (*dismisses police*): The following day the talks and whispers about psychiatrists – psychologists and their philosophy. (*Off, church clock chiming twelve.*) Time up?

JPW: No!

MAN: My – outbursts – are taking me by surprise. I don't know where the next one will lead me.

JPW: Yes! I mean to say, for a time, I started to play with the traffic. I mean, the startling thing, deliberately. Like a stiff-necked toreador in streets of highly dangerous traffic! I may have been a bull-fighter in a past life.

MAN: I want to sing.

JPW (*at the window*): Where are they all going? But all in my past needless to say, now that I have found my Helen.

MAN: I want to sing.

JPW (*continues absently*): That's one way of putting it.

MAN: I want to sing!

JPW: That's what I thought you said out there earlier.

MAN: Like Gigli. He was a tenor.

JPW: Why not Caruso?

MAN: It's Gigli.

JPW: Ah, we must not aim too high.

MAN (*sharply*): I've read one or two bits of snob things about Gigli.

JPW: I agree. He was emotional, was he?

MAN: Caruso is another thing.

JPW: Check. You want to sing, like Gigli, inverted commas.

MAN: No inverted commas.

JPW: Cut inverted commas, how much do you drink?

MAN: You don't understand.

JPW: Oh, I understand –

MAN: Drink is not –

JPW: Excuse me! I marked your grandiose remark, 'I know more about life than the lot of them put together'. What is that? And what is it indicative of? It is the statement of an alcoholic, my friend.

MAN: Drink is not a problem to me.

JPW: Exactly! Increase in alcohol tolerance. Excuse me! Inability to discuss problem, grandiose statements and aggressive behaviour, memory blackouts? unreasonable resentments, physical deterioration, loss of weight? vague spiritual desires – nearly finished – inability to initiate action – Enough? Alibis exhausted, defeat admitted? desire for recovery. How much do you drink?

MAN: I'm – a – very – poor – drinker, Mr King.

JPW: The night of the long knives –

MAN: Drink has nothing to –

JPW: Wine and those sleeping pills, lethal. People in America jumping out of windows on wings of Mandrax.

MAN: I often forget drink for three-four-five nights running!

JPW: I'm sorry – I enjoy a challenge, and this is a challenging one – but – But! – if we are to get to our objective, to sing, we have enough layers to destratify without being hampered by toxic liquids. So all drink out. Give it a try? – Good man. Now, tell me everything . . . Except your name.

MAN *toys with his hat for a moment.*

Yes, it becomes you . . . Place, time, date of birth is always a good starting point.

MAN: I was born with a voice and little else.

JPW: Naked we came into the world.

MAN: We were very poor.

JPW: What did your father do?

MAN: A cobbler.

JPW: Making or mending them? It could be significant.

MAN: He started by making them but factory-made shoes soon put paid to that.

JPW: Where was this?

MAN: Recanati.

JPW: Recan?

MAN: Ati.

JPW: What county is that in?

MAN: Recanati is in Italy.

JPW: Italian born?

MAN: My hair was a lot darker some years ago.

JPW: And your height.

MAN: Yeh.

JPW: And your frame. Quite Italianate.

MAN: And quite in the shape of a tenor's frame.

JPW: I can see that now.

MAN: I read it somewhere, tenors tend to be short and round for glandular reasons.

JPW: Interesting biological detail.

MAN: While for bassos – basses – they tend to be tall and thin – the same law applies but only in reverse.

JPW: Isn't that interesting?

MAN: It seems that only baritones are in the happy position of being normal.

JPW: And since the tenor usually plays the hero, this arrangement is all rather unfortunate.

MAN: Yeh.

JPW: What's your star?

MAN: Star!

JPW: Where exactly is Recan–?

MAN: Ati.

JPW: Small town? Me too. But yes?

MAN: Sing us a song, Benimillo, the people used to say. I knew all the pop songs and, as you know, all the famous arias are part of our – our culture.

JPW: Got your first name.

MAN: It was a pet name.

JPW: Benimillo.

MAN: I wasn't a great boy soprano but I was the best around. Another thing I read, the really good alto boy sopranos tend to develop later as bassos or baritones, so not being that alto – although good – I had it there as well.

JPW: As an indication that your future was to be a tenor. The clouds are beginning to clear at last, Benimillo.

MAN: I sang in the choir, of course.

JPW: Me too.

MAN: But this was a fine choir. We sang Gregorian Chant and, oh, all sorts of things like the sacred music of Rossini and Gounod.

JPW: Thieving Magpie.

MAN: The singing master treated me very affectionately.

JPW: Yes. A queer bird the cuckoo, he sits in the grass his wings neatly folded, his beak up his – go on. (*He finishes a drink behind* MAN's *back.*)

MAN: I was taken out of class at the age of nine to sing with the twelve, fourteen-year olds.

JPW: Aha! What time is it?

MAN: Quarter past twelve. We gave concerts.

JPW: You sang solo.

MAN: Short pieces. And sometimes we even got paid.

JPW: When did your voice break?

MAN: I was fifteen –

JPW: Good. Well, let's see what we have now.

MAN: But my voice hadn't broke. And then, one day, these three young men come all the way from Macerata, and all because of me.

JPW: What did they want?

MAN: They wanted me to dress up as a

girl and sing the soprano role in an operetta.

JPW: Strangers?

MAN: 'Angelica's Elopement'.

JPW: Strangers?

MAN: No. But such a thing was out of the question, my mother said.

JPW: I should think so.

MAN: No. But she said she was sorry they'd made such a long journey for nothing but 'twas their own fault and then she sent them packing

JPW: Good. Well now, when did the old voice break so that we can start motoring?

MAN: But they weren't to be put off that easy.

JPW: They came back?

MAN: They came back, pleading. They said I'd have a share of the profits. Well, my father said – He was still alive at the time. After all, he said, there's no great harm in it. Not that my mother ever paid much heed to him. She always looked to Abramo, my eldest brother. Abramo was the real figure of authority in our house.

JPW: What did Abramo say?

MAN: Well, my mother got a little surprise because, after thinking, Abramo said that he personally couldn't see anything in it to frown about. (*A smile of minor triumph.*) Hah?

JPW: Very interesting, truly, Benimillo, but I think I have now got sufficient data on that area.

MAN: No –

JPW: So many other areas to audit.

MAN: No –

JPW: For instance, I played Yum-Yum, 'The Mikado' you know?, at boarding school, and came out of the experience comparatively unscathed.

MAN: The next few weeks were fraught, fraught with excitement. Trips to Macerata, rehearsals, and we played, not in a grimey little hall, but in the municipal theatre. Someone had to push me on the stage. Then, suddenly,

everything was alright and I sauntered back and forth with me parasol singing 'Passigiando un anno fa'. I couldn't hardly believe my ears that all the cries of 'Bis! Bis!' was really for me.

JPW: Bis.

MAN: To tell the God's honest truth, I felt ashamed like, getting so much more of the clapping than the others.

JPW: Your accent– you must have been very young when you came to this country.

MAN: But I'd filled the hall with my voice, held the crowd. They understood. And, I thought, I can do it again. I will do it again.

JPW: But it was on to the building trade.

MAN: I suppose the experience made me – giddy. But I don't know. 'Twas more than that. And 'twasn't the clapping. Like, you can talk forever, but singing. Singing, d'yeh know? The only possible way to tell people.

JPW: What?

MAN (*shrugs, he does not know*): . . . Who you are? . . . But Abramo said, you may have been to – to . . .

JPW: Macerata.

MAN: Macerata, singing and playacting, but that doesn't mean you forget your manners or the straits this family is in, and the job I had to look after.

JPW: In the building trade?

MAN (*ire rising*): In the – what? – No! – The shop – messenger-boy – the local pharmacia, whatever the (*fuck that is*) – A shop boy, messenger-boy, dogsbody – my brother was a tyrant!

JPW: Good! Well, let us see now –

MAN (*harsh, intense, impotent hatred*): And the man I worked for, *he* was an alcoholic, a quack, a paratise, a failure in everything, ate rat poison one night and I came to this country shortly after!

JPW: . . , I mean, that it is time, and I wanted to sum up.

MAN: Sum up *what*?

JPW: That you are undergoing severe depression and –

MAN: What does that mean, depression?

JPW: You can look it up for yourself.

MAN: Everything mean and low!

JPW: Dispirited, humbled, yes, brought low.

MAN: Everything mean and low!

JPW: Reduction in pitch of voice?

MAN: Do you mean I'm unhappy?

JPW: I should imagine so.

MAN: Then I'm unhappy.

JPW: That's good: anger, let it all come out. That is what I shall be aiming at.

MAN: What have you been writing there?

JPW: Confidential.

MAN: What have you been writing down?

JPW: Your file. Unethical –

MAN *snaps the sheet of paper.*

A matter between your GP and myself.

MAN (*reading*): 'Facts. There are too many facts in the world.'

JPW: Interesting observation of yours.

MAN: 'Fiction. Fantasy' – (*He looks at JPW who averts his eyes.*) . . . 'Bis'.

JPW: Encore?

MAN: 'Towards the end of the session he smiled.'

JPW: You did. We made progress.

MAN: 'Pot of jam, tea, saccharin.'

JPW: I do not take sugar. You might not think it, but I am still vain.

MAN: Do you think I'm a fool?

JPW: No. And I am not one either.

MAN: You were summing up.

JPW: That you are deeply unhappy – presently –

MAN: Aren't you?

JPW: And psychotic.

MAN: Me?

JPW: Yes.

MAN: What's psychotic?

JPW: Out of control

MAN: Is that so? (*Face contorted in impotent hatred*). Anything else?

JPW: You do not like what you are.

MAN: Better than not knowing who or what I am!

JPW: Another appointment in town, actually running late, but let me see. Yes, I could manage, fortunately, another session tomorrow, same time – well, perhaps a little later. Twelve o'clock?

MAN: I don't think so. (*Going out.*)

JPW: I can make you sing! And remember –

MAN *is gone*

. . . all drink out. (*He polishes off the remainder of his vodka*) He's crazy.

He sticks a book in his pocket, is collecting up the money. MONA *is entering with some fruit and cigarettes for him.*

MONA: Well, lover! Who was that I met on the stairs? (*Glancing at the couch.*) How about a session?

He is already gone out the door. She puts down the fruit and the cigarettes.

MONA: No joy here, productive or otherwise! Here, there, elsewhere, where? Perhaps tonight. So, little one, shall we go look at the sea? Too boring, cold, polluted? Bewley's then, again: tea and cakes. Or, the ezzo (*zoo*)? cinema? to see more shite. Ahm, we'll ah, we'll ah . . . be talking about it on the way home. (*Surveying room.*) Out of the womb to the wall-to-wall carpeting of the tomb. Aa, fuck it, child, let's go somewhere.

She takes the hand of an imagined child and is leaving. Lights fading, up sound: Gigli singing 'O Paradiso'.

Scene Two

Off, church clock chiming twelve. JPW *huddled in bed, in a drunken stupor, asleep. Bell on outer door ringing, silhouette,* MAN *coming to office door, knocking . . .*

MAN: Mr King! . . . Mr King! . . .

Silhouette pacing to and fro for a few moments, eventually leaving. Lights fading, up sound: Gigli continuing 'O Paradiso'.

Scene Three

JPW *on the phone.*

JPW: . . . Same answer I suppose? (*He nods gravely at her reply.*) . . . 'Bye. What? . . . Oh, couple of interviews in town and . . . Oh, what am I doing now? . . . At this very moment? . . . Stack of letters in front of me requiring attention and – you know? Very busy . . . No, I'm still here . . . Frost again? . . . What? . . . I try . . . I promise . . . I promise . . . 'Bye.

He puts phone down, goes to window, lets up the blind, looking out over city.

'Please, please, don't phone me again' . . . I try. Helen.

Then reacting to someone watching his window from the street. And into action: phone apparatus re-adjusted, empty vodka bottle on bed dumped, bed reconverted, extinguishes cigarette, spectacles for effect, etc., unlocks the door, opens it, and sits in confident attitude. Church clock chiming two. MAN arrives and stands in doorway, abject.

This is a fine time of day! Come in.

MAN *continues in the doorway, abject.*

But when I say twelve o'clock, I mean twelve o'clock! Come in!

MAN *comes in; his attitude appears numbed; JPW becoming unnerved and through the following searching for his battery-operated shaver, finds it eventually, finds the batteries are dead . . .*

And how was your evening? Jolly? On the town? A trout from your stream? . . . Well, I have to shave. A beard is all very fine but bloody irritating stuff at this stage. What do you do in the evenings?

MAN: I don't go out.

JPW: Where did I leave the blasted thing?

MAN: Where does a man go to?

JPW: That is a very intelligent question, my friend.

MAN: Are you married?

JPW (*looks at him for a moment*): . . . What?

MAN: A saint is she?

JPW: A saint is she yes, I must admit she is pretty special. Irish colleen, apron, you know?, darns my socks, that kind of thing. I am very fond of her and she is very fond of chintz.

MAN: A saint is she?

JPW: Standardised activity, routine trivia, but I must confess to a lure about certain domestic ceremonials. And on the silver salver a platonic aphrodisiac, two loving cups of secure cocoa as I lead her up the stairs at night. (*Finds shaver.*) Ah, I'm blessed.

MAN: Children.

JPW: Two. But do you know what I was thinking, Benimillo? Some boy sopranos develop with no voices at all, at all. And manage somehow.

MAN: A boy and a girl.

JPW: And I met a man last evening, a creditable bar-room tenor, and the startling thing, do you know his ambition? The confident obsession of it in his Thursday-night eyes. That in four years' time he is going to make the rank of dumper-driver. Makes one think. (*At the window.*) Yes, I am married. A boy just like his mother and a girl the image of me. And I have often thought – what I wouldn't give! – to own a fleet of JCBs. Tangibles. That is where fortune and glory lies. To sit back and watch them, biting lumps out of the arse of the earth for me. Jesus, the batteries are gone in this again! I must wake up somehow.

MAN: Why don't you get a lead for it?

JPW: And that is another very intelligent question.

Searching for towel, toothpaste etc., in and out of the washroom, his singing falsetto.

(*Sings.*) 'Oh pray make no mistake we are not shy, we're really wide awake –'

Terrible life singing.

MAN (*silently*): No.

JPW: 'We really know our worth, the sun and I'. Castrato. But it happened out riding. It was either have the operation, or die. (*Going out to washroom.*)

MAN (*alone, quietly*): I built a fire at home last night and burned all the toys in the house.

JPW (*off*): What?

MAN: What am I do do?

JPW (*off*): What?

JPW *now watching* MAN *from washroom doorway.*

MAN: Stupid, numbed, guilty, worthless, finished. Everything so stale, so mean and low.

JPW (*off*): You may smoke if you wish.

MAN: Stupid, numbed, guilty. Finished? Naaw!

JPW (*comes breezing in*): And I spent a night with a contralto once. Actually I was chasing the cellist, ended up with the contralto. Marathon struggle, exceeding large lady, every pound the prima donna – Hmm? (*Offering* MAN *a cigarette.* MAN *shakes his head.*) But I struck oil. (*Offers cigarette again.*) Sure?

MAN (*shakes his head*): Do you live here, Mr King?

JPW: No, what?

MAN: I envy it.

JPW: I don't. I use the place, of course, obviously, for, you know? But no. What?

MAN: Then where do you live?

JPW: Nothing very large, of course, but clematis round the door, that sort of dwelling. Perhaps in one of your own sylvan developments, what?

MAN: With the wife?

JPW: She does not have to darn my socks, of course, but that is her nature. Even when they have got no holes in them! (*He laughs.*) . . . Hey, Benimillo, does Quasimodo ring a bell? Quasimodo. Charles Laughton. Quasimodo.

MAN: The hunchback?

JPW: Yes, of Notre Dame, does he ring a bell? (*Mimes.*) Ring a bell.

MAN: Oh.

JPW: There's nothing staler than death, my friend.

MAN (*suddenly wild*): And what about me?

JPW *uncomprehending.*

I! Me! I! What I Want!

JPW: And that is why we are here.

MAN: What I feel!

JPW: Check.

MAN: Inside!

JPW: Yes! And now to make sure I am not dealing with a crow-complex we shall have a song.

MAN *growls to himself.*

Well, to sing like Gigli in six easy lessons.

MAN: He's the devil!

JPW: He's the . . . Oh for God's sake, Benimillo, snap out of it.

MAN: What! That's a – a stupid, ridiculous thing to say. D'yeh think I'd be this way if I could help it? When I listen to him – I-can't-stop-listening-to-him! Fills me. The – things, the – things – inside. Tense, everything more intense. And I listen carefully. And it's beautiful – But it's screaming! – And it's longing. Longing for what? I don't know whether it's keeping me sane or driving me crazy . . . You may laugh.

JPW: I am not laughing.

MAN: Or is it mocking me?

JPW: Music hath charms to –

MAN: Naaw, whoever said that is a fool. And it has affected everything 'round me. A record! A Christmas present! I need to listen to him now!

JPW: Disconnect him.

MAN: I achieved things, boy. I come from nothing. Or what does it want me to do? Fly!

JPW: Stop listening to him.

MAN: I'll see it through. My wife is near

nervous breakdown. She's barely holding on. She says I look like an old man. Hah?

JPW: And so you do.

MAN: She looks like an old woman. She was a princess. You should have seen her. Even three months ago. She's holding on for me she says, not the child. The child too, but why on earth for me? And I burned all his toys last night. I rooted them out of every corner. And I'm so proud of him. I see him watching me sometimes. He's almost nine. I watch him sometimes too, secretly, and wonder will I write him a letter. Or take him for a little walk, my arm around his shoulders. Because, though he's nearly nine, and a boy, he would still allow me put my arm around his shoulders. My son. And explain to him that I don't matter. That it would be better if I disappeared.

JPW: Ah, Mr . . .

MAN: And sometimes I wish them things (*dead*) that I don't want to wish them, things that are maybe going to turn out unlucky.

JPW: Ah, Mr . . .

MAN: My wife come down last night. Nightdress, long hair. I pretended I didn't hear her come in or that she was watching me. And I kept listening to the music. Then she come and stood beside my chair. Smiling. And she said, what are you listening to? I use the headphones at night. Elgar, I said. I don't know why I said that because the only thing I listen to is him. And. You off I said. To bed. And she said yes, it's ten past one heighho. And. You coming up she said. And I said, in a little I said. And. Then she knelt down and put her head on my knees. And then she said talk to me. Talk to me, talk to me, please love talk to me. And I couldn't think of a single thing to say. And then she said, I love you so much. And I said I love you too . . . but not out loud. And. Then she got up. And then she said pull yourself together, what's the matter with you, for God's sake get a grip on yourself, pull yourself together. She was trembling. She'd let go for a moment. And then

she said goodnight. When she left I stood up. Out of respect. I knew she would've stopped in the hall. She usually does. Just stands there for a few moments. Before going up. And. Then it come out. My roar. Fuck you, fuck you . . . fuck you. (*Though delivered quietly and the intense emotion contained, tears have started down the man's face during the speech.*)

JPW: Ah, Mr . . . I'm out of my depth . . . This organisation . . . Steve, our founder, leader, came over and set up this office. Though I have always wanted to achieve something, I couldn't do even that much on my own. They sent me over here. But even they have forgotten me. And I have forgotten them. I think it is likely they shipped Steve back to the States. I do not even know if we are still in existence.

MAN: Then-why-do-you-stay-on-in-this-terrible-country-then!

JPW (*a gesture to the window. 'Helen', changes his mind and follows with the peculiarly defensive reply under the circumstances*): That's – that is my affair! I'm out of my depth.

They speak simultaneously:

MAN: No, you're not –

JPW: I'm out of my depth!

MAN: No, you're not.

JPW: I have no answers, I'm at my wits' end –

MAN: No, you're not, no you're not –

JPW: Good grief, trying to work things out, all my life, for myself.

Until:

MAN: Your Helen, your dwelling, your –

JPW: Yes, my – that is none of your business!

MAN: I'm happy with you.

JPW: There is no organisation!

MAN: I'm happy with you, Mr King.

JPW: A real, recognised, qualified, university-trained psychiatrist you need.

MAN *rolling his head.*

What have you against them?

MAN: They don't know! – Philosophy! And people like them – I've dealt with them – I've had them on the building sites – Worse than their elders – finished, corrupt before they've even started – walking fast in pinstripe suits – that's all they know – Or fucked-up by too much education – That's all they know!

JPW: They can see patterns.

MAN: I'm happy with you.

They speak simultaneously:

JPW: (*'No'*) I don't mind making a fast buck –

MAN: I have a lot of time for instinct –

JPW: I don't mind telling you I need the shillings –

MAN: Always used instinct –

JPW: But, in fairness, I draw the line. I am not, though you might think it, a ponce.

Until:

MAN: Instinct, my strength, boy. Unerring instinct for the right man for the job.

JPW: This is not a job!

MAN: I'll get to the root of this, I'll see it through, my way. I've never been beaten – Oh, they tried, but I left a few cripples around the place. I've taken on, done business with the big – (*Whispers.*) the biggest in the land – and there was nothing he, or they, could teach little me. Never been beaten, a survivor, and this isn't going to beat me either.

JPW: Gently for a second. For what it is worth, my opinion: in any game it is dangerous taking up arms against an unknown enemy.

MAN (*hand in pocket*): And if all comes to all, I have the trump card.

JPW: Gently, for a second. Are we talking about singing? I mean, can you be serious?

MAN: Oh, I'm always serious –

JPW: To sing!

MAN: I could never afford to be anything but serious!

JPW: Benimillo –

MAN: I'm so serious –

JPW: Benimillo! –

MAN: You look out – you-look-out! – cause I'm going to get you too!

JPW (*a silent*): Well-well.

MAN: So is my time up for today?

JPW: I should imagine it is. I have some meditating to do.

MAN: So what time tomorrow?

JPW: Tomorrow is Saturday, I do not work weekends.

MAN: I'll pay you in advance? – For the remaining four sessions. Cash or – it'll have to be a cheque.

JPW: And you want a session on Sunday? Well-well. That was not a very kind thing to say to a friend, Benimillo.

MAN: How much?

JPW: Double-time for Saturday and Sunday.

MAN: How much?

JPW: A round figure?

MAN: A hundred pounds.

JPW: Gosh! A hundred pounds!

MAN: I'll make it out pay cash.

JPW: Your desperation is fantastic.

MAN: Always conscious of money but-I-was-never interested in it.

JPW: Yeh.

MAN: I'll make it . . .?

JPW: Yes? . . . A hundred is fine, and a cheque is fine, and the banks are still open.

MAN: What time tomorrow?

JPW: Your choice.

MAN: You'll be here?

JPW: State the time.

MAN: You'll be here?

JPW: I'll be here.

MAN (*about to hand over the cheque, remembers*): I'll be back with cash in two minutes.

MAN goes out.

JPW: Nearly got your second name, Benimillo! . . . Jesus Christ!

JPW reflective, then a short kicking dance, two feet off the ground at the same time, reflective again, an idea; he uncovers a classified telephone directory, finds a number, adjustment to telephone apparatus . . .

Hospitals, hospitals. What am I doing? – He's crazy! St Anne's, administration, nurses' residence, X-ray department. St Andrew's. No. St Godolph's unusual one, administration, nurses' – ah! (*Raps out a number.*) Psychiatric department, please . . . Good afternoon. The psychiatrist in charge, please . . . his assistant then . . . any psychiatrist . . . yes, an appointment . . . no, for my brother . . . for today . . . next month! . . . couldn't she see me tomorow? . . . I know tomorrow is Saturday, Miss, but I have got my brother outside, now, literally tied up with ropes in the boot of the car . . . Miss, I'm a practising GP and this is not a case for your casualty department . . . Madam, I am sitting on a barrel of gun powder, can-you-help-me? . . . Monday. What time? . . . That's very early . . . I said that is fine . . . What? . . . Oh, Mickeleen O'Loughlin. (*He puts phone down.*)

MAN returns and puts money on the desk.

MAN: Noon tomorrow. And you had better be here. Do you understand that?

JPW Striking pose head to head with MAN across the desk.

JPW: Bring your pistols! I'll bring the booze!

Up music, quick fade – final section of 'O Paradiso' to conclude this scene.

Scene Four

Gigli's 'O Paradiso' again.
JPW and MONA in bed swapping a bottle of vodka. JPW drinking hard to fortify himself. On the floor beside the bed some new books, a sheet of notes an a newly-drawn-up chart. Some groceries on the desk.

Ideally, MONA is a big woman, though not large of bust as the text indicates. Her moods can alternate as quickly as her thoughts, but her vitality, generosity and seemingly celebratory nature allow her to hold a 'down' mood only fleetingly. She is about thirty-eight. She is dressed in a white slip.

MONA: You're not listening to me.

He nods.

I shouldn't have dropped in?

He nods.

You're bored now?

He nods. She kicks him or whatever.

And-I-Was-Ravenous. So I dashed out and took my god-child to her ballet class. Dashed back home. Pacing the floor again. What had I to do now? *And-I-Was-Still-Ravenous* – for something. So I ate three eggs, then two yoghurts: still wondering. What'll I do now, what'll I have now? So I thought I'll chance you.

JPW: Well, I am going to see this thing through too.

MONA: You're not listening to me!

JPW: I am. He may even shoot me if I don't.

MONA: Who?

JPW: Benimillo. A practical man, like my father. But this practical man is declaring that the romantic kingdom *is* of this world.

MONA: And that's all you were doing last night, reading?

JPW: I *want* him to prove it. I am contracted to assist him.

MONA: If I had known.

JPW: Do you see what I mean? And I have been up all night. And I am forty-six.

MONA: I could have come over – to assist you.

JPW: And I had it all figured out at one point. They said I'd never achieve anything. I got very excited.

She is lying on top of him or snuggling up to him

. . . Pardon? No! You should not be

doing this to me.

MONA: Seducing you, lover?

JPW: Yes.

MONA: It's freezing in here.

JPW: It was all crystal clear.

MONA (*under the bedclothes*): Nothing much happening down here, my friend.

JPW: No! No! You should not! And bringing those – those groceries! – over here.

MONA: You never talk about my problems anymore.

JPW: Now I have forgotten it all.

MONA (*to herself*): Nobody does.

JPW: What on earth am I to do?

MONA (*to herself*): Keep on dreaming.

JPW: I must keep it on a conversational level at all costs. But how does one do that?

MONA: You keep on talking.

JPW: Pardon?

MONA: Keep on – (*Gestures 'talking'.*)

JPW: Yes! Because, I mean to say, I am not *that* afraid of him.

MONA: And shock them if you can.

JPW: Yes, I'm sure he's a Catholic

She laughs.

Are you a Catholic?

MONA (*nods*): And I pray.

JPW: What is original sin?

MONA: Fuck original sin.

JPW: Existential guilt.

MONA: What about my problems!

JPW: What problems?

MONA: I'm a subject.

JPW: You jump into bed as soon as you come in that door.

MONA: That's my problem.

JPW: I was lucky to escape the other day.

MONA: That's why I came early this morning. (*She starts to dress.*)

JPW: What are you doing?

MONA: Another port of call.

JPW: Where to?

MONA: Oh? A man. Does funny things to me. Are you jealous? You: fat chance.

JPW: Don't go yet.

MONA: Alright . . . My chin is all sore, it is all red? What'll my husband say? I'm annoyed now I didn't think of batteries for your shaver.

JPW (*absently*): Did you think of a pot of jam?

MONA (*solemn nod 'yes' and followed by a solemn tone – of weariness? – as she gets back into bed*): But I have to collect my god-daughter. Then to the doctor.

JPW: What-is-life?

MONA: Life, my friend, is bouncing back. But, I suppose I was lucky to get in here at all, hmm? The bars are going up around town against old Mona. And some *curtain* is being drawn. Jimmy. Promise me something. That you'll let me down gently.

JPW: What are you talking about?

MONA: Now that you ask. I'm not quite sure. Or where I am or what I'm at. I know there's someone else – I've always known it – but I'm not too bad, am I?

JPW (*defensively*): What someone else?

MONA: But I know it. But I *know* it! Look at you now: eyes like a wounded – nun.

JPW: I'm forty-six.

MONA: Great man for your age alright. Who is she? – I mean just for interest's sake.

JPW: I'm very flattered.

MONA: I'm twenty-eight. Thirty-eight. And nothing to show for it yet. When I get into bed with you I say right Mona, down to work, fifteen times today.

JPW: We did it twice the time before last.

MONA: *My* doing. And you're only a baby – all men are babies – and I'd hate to have big tits.

JPW: I never said –

MONA: Some men do! (*Then she*

laughs.) In the past. Promise. Like a month's notice.

JPW: 'In the past'. And all your 'dashing' around town at night? 'But I *know* it'.

MONA: I always try here first.

JPW: Well, you shouldn't.

MONA: Well, what is it about me, tell me? – as against Miss-whoever-she-is. And she doesn't look after you very well, does she? (*She indicates the room.*)

JPW: You are a respectable married woman!

Then they laugh. Then she becomes grave.

MONA: Don't laugh at me. You don't know what it's like.

JPW: What?

MONA (*mutters*): Good old Mona. *And,* I don't like being used.

JPW: Yes, well, but, Mona, I sometimes feel –

MONA: That's the first time you used my name today.

JPW: Yes, but, well, I sometimes feel that you are possibly, I mean to say, using me. (*She nods gravely.*) I mean, the interesting thing, who picked up whom that evening in the supermarket?

MONA: At the health-food counter.

JPW: I have often wondered.

MONA: My magician. And you are so gentle. I'll give you the money to have that phone reconnected.

JPW: I'm a wage-earner now, I have a job.

MONA: Suit yourself. Only, sometimes, I wish I could talk to you. Hear that posh voice of yours.

JPW: I have not got a posh voice.

MONA: 'I have not got a –'

JPW: Mona!

MONA: Alright, you have got a real west of Ireland accent.

JPW: . . . What's wrong with this famous god-child of yours, Karen?

MONA: Karen Marie (*Maree*)

JPW: Karen Marie.

MONA: I'm going to the doctor.

JPW: What's wrong with you?

MONA: I fancy the doctor.

JPW: I wouldn't put it past you.

MONA: Where would you put it? . . . You don't like those remarks.

He gets it and laughs.

But, at least, you deign to talk to me when I'm here. Not like some. And not like that string of misery I have at home. (*She grunts in imitation of her husband.*) I'm leaving him. Don't worry, not because of you. (*Laughs.*) And I have him worn out too. (*Sighs.*) I should have married a farmer.

JPW: Six children.

MONA: Double it. Now you're getting close. Here, I'll give you a laugh. You know how I take that god-child everywhere with me? But-Can-I-Stop-Her-Dawdling-Behind! We were shopping during the week and we had to go through the men's wear department to get to the ladies' wear, and suddenly this voice, 'Madam! Madam!' This poor shop-assistant, eighty, if he was a day. And I looked around for Karen-Marie. And you know shop-dummies? Well, there she was, innocent as you like, looking up at their faces, unzipping their flies and putting her hand inside. 'Madam! Madam!' And I'm shouting . . . There's someone outside.

Silhouette of MAN arriving outside, tapping the door with his shoe.

Is that him?

JPW: Stay where you are.

MONA: Ah, Jimmy –

JPW: I shan't be long, Benimillo! (*Silhouette moving away*.) No, let him wait – Bloody hell – he's early. What am I going to say to him? Unzipping their flies and putting their hand inside . . . . putting her hand inside.

MONA (*continues in a whisper, dressing hurriedly*): 'Madam! Madam!' And I'm shouting 'Karen-Marie! Karen-Marie!' 'Madam! Madam' 'Karen-Marie! Karen-Marie!' And says Karen-Marie –

(*To* JPW:) Don't be looking at me. (*Dressing.*) 'They're only dummies', she said, 'they have no willies.' Well laugh!

JPW: They have no willies. (*Putting on his trousers, etc.*)

MONA: And the other women about were in hysterics.

JPW: And what happened then?

MONA: And what happened then . . . (*She appears peculiarly lost for a moment.*) I think I'm going crazy. Am I forgetting anything?

Off, church clock chiming twelve.

MONA: Jesus! – Twelve o'clock! – How do I get out of here?

JPW: He's not my wife.

MONA: You haven't got a wife. (*Adjusting her bodice, referring to her breasts.*) If it fits in your mouth it's big enough. See yeh, get the phone mended will yeh, see yeh.

He lets her out and shuts the door. He is smoking, drinking; he leaves the bed unconverted, moves books on floor under the bed, opens the door on the last chime of the church clock, strikes a pose with his newly drawn-up chart, his back to the door, and waits.
    MAN *comes to stand in the doorway; he is carrying a large cardboard box. He looks pleased with himself this morning.*

MAN: Can I come in?

JPW (*curt*): Come in.

MAN: I arrived a bit early I'm afraid. I did a little shopping. Can I come in?

JPW: It must be spoken three times. Come in.

MAN: I couldn't ring the bell because of these. I brought the pistols. Can I put it here? . . . Hah? . . . Hah? . . . It's easy enough put together . . . Hah?

MAN *chuckling 'Hah', producing a new record-player from the box, and a record.*
    JPW *a little thrown, surprised and resentful of this move, but trying to contain himself.*

JPW: You mean to say you bought that?

MAN: Hah? . . . the wife? (*Mona*)

JPW: No, not the wife, Benimillo. Drink? While I am *waiting* for you.

MAN: Hah? Thanks, yes, why not, please.

JPW: Oh?

MAN: Weekend. She was wearing a ring.

JPW: She wasn't! Begod! Another man's wife, Benimillo, are you shocked?

MAN: Good luck!

JPW: She's a Catholic.

MAN: And what does your own wife think about all this in your sylvan dwelling?

JPW *reacts angrily, sweeping the groceries off the desk into drawers or wherever.*
    . . . I didn't mean to offend you or . . . Wha'?

JPW: Ah, sure man dear alive, a mac, sure I know well you didn't sure – And that machine set you back a few quid, five or six hundred?

MAN: Are you having an affair, Mr King?

JPW: She may think so.

MAN: Oh now, that's a bit chauvinist.

JPW (*silent 'chauvinist'*): What did you think of her?

MAN: A fine big woman.

JPW: But her tits – you don't fancy big tits then?

MAN: Is there a power point somewhere?

JPW: I knew this Irish chap once had a big thing about (*Mimes.*) round electric light switches.

MAN (*finds the powerpoint*): Here we are.

JPW: Ah but sure if it fits in your mouth it's big enough.

MAN: Anything more is a waste. (*In reaction to JPW's surprise.*) That's what we used to say alright. If it fits in your mouth it's big enough, anything more is a waste.

JPW: But, but – personally, Benimillo, personally, big or small, they are startling things, and I am always astonished at how casually the ladies themselves take them for granted.

MAN: There we are. (*Set up.*)

JPW: Would you agree with that observation?

MAN (*switches on machine – orchestral opening bars of 'O Paradiso'*): D'yeh mind?

JPW: I do.

MAN (*cueing to another track*): No, not this first one, it starts with 'O Paradiso' but there's a piece here –

JPW: I said I do mind!

MAN: Wha'?

JPW: I said no, Benimillo, no! (*He switches off the machine.*)

MAN: I just want you to listen to him.

JPW: I said no! You want to listen to him or you want to sing like him, which? Sit down. We have work to do. Look at this chart please.

MAN (*placatory*): I enjoy our meetings, Mr King.

JPW: You see this circle here, the most perfect of shapes, the cosmic womb, the perfect state, the clear pool of being. We travel down this line –

MAN: I look forward to them.

JPW: To our second pool, existence, the here and now. Again the most perfect of shapes, but look at what is inside. A mess.

MAN: I enjoy them.

JPW: Circles within circles, concentric and eccentric, squiggles, swirls of objects, and at the bottom, sediment, this dark area here, despair. Our problem, to achieve the state of clear which exists here, in our second pool, here. But, paradoxically, it is from this dark area, this rising darkness of our despair that the solution is to derive, if – if! – we can get it to rise to cover the whole pool and blot out our squiggles and circles and what-nots. Good.

MAN: What's that third pool?

JPW: Indeed. And I should be grateful if you did not interrupt further. The areas we shall be going into from here on in are not without risk, and will demand not only your concentration, but that courage required for an encounter of a most strange and singular kind.

MAN: You're having me on.

JPW: Pardon?

MAN: Aw.

JPW: 'Aw'?

MAN: Naaw.

JPW: 'Naaw'? You are not saying, I hope, that you thought the simple problem you have set us would be solved in the traditional way? I mean by sitting down together and playing that game called Slobs. The winner proves himself to be the most sentimental player and becomes King Slob by dealing, at the most unexpected moment, a sudden judas punch, or an emotional kick in the genitals to his opponent, thereby *getting* him. Problem solved.

MAN: I was out of sorts yesterday.

JPW: But we had a good night last night, had we, slept well?

MAN (*almost silently*): No.

JPW: The three aspects which we shall concentrate on today are, one and two, the twin paralysing demons, your existential guilt, and the I-am-who-am syndrome. And three, despair. Then, if you are up to it, we shall over the next three days set to possibilising that quiet power of the possible waiting within you.

MAN: Naaw, aw.

JPW: 'Naaw – aw' again! Explain yourself. Ah! You are impatient to ask what is your natural existential guilt.

MAN: Guilt – exist – I am not guilty of anything.

Speaking simultaneously.

JPW: Heard you yesterday, imprisoned, numbed, guilty.

MAN: Survival! – What am I guilty of, survival? D'yeh know what's going on out there?

JPW: The point is you feel guilty.

MAN: And innocent at the same time!

JPW: That's good. Just like Adam when he got the boot.

MAN (*silently*): Adam!

JPW: What have I done he said to God, I only – But God said, out, out!

MAN: You're having me on!

JPW: But what had Adam done? No, it was not a deed. Adam did not lose his head over Eve in the Garden, he lost his tail – when he bit the apple. He *gained* a head, knowledge – Tree of Knowledge – a little of which, one bite, is a dangerous thing. He started thinking, and consciousness – *thinking* – and self-consciousness crept in, which is existential guilt, which is original sin.

MAN: I don't know what you're talking about!

JPW: Indeed, I contend, that it was much later that the screwing started. Mind-numbing stuff to stop those very feelings of simultaneous innocence and guilt, and, naturally, finding themselves out in the cold, simply to keep themselves warm, the creatures.

MAN: What's this got to do with it?

JPW: On to clearing the jungle, developing it, mind-numbing drudgery to stop the pain – what had they lost, what was the beauty they were longing for? On to milking the goats, cutting the grass, trying to get Cain to toe a more conservative and respectable line, standardised activity, routine trivia, looking for the new security.

MAN: *You* don't know what you're talking about!

JPW (*confronting* MAN): And all the time trying to obliterate that side of their nature that was innocent and beautiful, as if it was the side that was vulgar, vicious, mean, ruthless, offensive, dangerous, obscene. Benimillo, what are you doing? . . . Benimillo!

MAN *has gone to record-player and cued in a track. He faces* JPW *squarely, a dangerous and warning attitude telling* JPW *not to interfere. Gigli singing 'Dai Campi, Dai Prati'. They listen to the complete aria.* MAN's *attitude softens through the aria and a few whimper-like sounds escape.* JPW *conceals his appreciation of the singing.*
At the conclusion of the aria, MAN *switches off the machine and waits with*

a childlike expectation for an appreciative reaction.

MAN: . . . Wha'? . . . Hah? . . . That's not my favourite, but because of that I thought you might like it best . . . Wha'? . . .

JPW: Did you have your tonsils out?

MAN: What? . . . I didn't! What did you think of him?

JPW: Sobs a bit much, doesn't he, pouts a bit much.

MAN: That's the snobbery I was talking about!

JPW: And those 'h' sounds.

MAN: King!

JPW (*has picked up the record sleeve*): Yes, Beniamino.

MAN (*muttering furiously*): Oh but the English, the English, what would they know anyway.

JPW: Do you know what he is singing?

MAN: You don't have to!

JPW: Do you understand the words?

MAN: You don't –

JPW: What opera was that piece from?

MAN: You don't have to know! I could always size a man up more from the sound he makes than from what he's saying.

JPW: Your unerring instinct. (*Looking at record sleeve.*) 'Mefistofele': Ah yes, he *is* the devil.

MAN: We were making little gold crosses over here when ye, over there, were still living in holes in the ground.

JPW: I do not doubt your word on it but what precisely is your point?

MAN: I hate yeh!

JPW: Sorry about that, old boy, but would we now choose to be superior if we could help it?

MAN: Oh, but very cold people the English, the British – Oh, and your Empire: that's located somewhere now in – what's them little islands called?

JPW: Oh, come, you can do better than that, you who have dealt and fenced and parried with the highest in the land. Have another drink, it will stimulate you. Here.

MAN *sends a chair careering across the room with a kick; he is about to smash his glass, and possibly* JPW *as well.*

MAN: Do you know who you're dealing with?

JPW: Be my guest (*smash the glass.*) . . . I find I am not afraid of you. Despite the path you have left behind you strewn with cripples – and corpses? Jail, hospital, or – (*Mimes shooting himself in the head.*) mean nothing to me either. But I have only two glasses remaining in the house, and if you smash that one, I shall certainly break this precious bottle over your head before you make a second move.

MAN (*a warning*): Don't try to take him (*Gigli*) away from me, Mr King.

JPW: On the contrary. I am beginning to find this project most exciting. *I* intend to see it through. You say similarly, but I have an instinct too, and something is bothering me about *your* commitment. (*He pours drinks.*) And further, if despair is to be our key, what am I to think when I see you arrive in here this morning – smiling?

MAN: To sing!

JPW: That's good. Repeat it.

MAN: To sing, to sing!

JPW: And I want you to go on repeating it. Yes, cheers! Because the most dangerous approach to our work from here-on-in is the half-longing half-frightened one. Look at our chart, please – the third pool, the one you asked about. One false step and not only do you miss your target but you end up out here, pool three, questionmark pool, banana-land.

MAN (*helping himself to another drink*): You'd know about it out there!

JPW: I am simply obliged to warn you.

MAN: Cheers-cheers-cheers!

JPW: And you may never come back.

MAN: What of it?

JPW: Indeed! (*Laughing, getting carried away with himself.*) You may never come back to the poxy, boring anchor

of this everyday world you have sold your soul for.

MAN: What of it?

JPW: The poxy boring anchor of this everyday world that others of us are shut out from!

MAN: What of it?

JPW: Indeed! The choice is yours. But I must be convinced of your commitment, and –

MAN: Wait a minute –

JPW: You are the one, to my mind, beginning to falter.

MAN: Wait a minute, what did you say?

JPW: What did I say?

MAN: There's something all along not making sense.

JPW: Well, of course, I have not as yet explained the paralysing I-am-who-am syndrome.

MAN: No. The poxy everyday world that others of us are shut out from.

JPW: Pardon?

MAN: This house of yours, sylvan dwelling – this wife of yours?

JPW: Allow me to complete my thesis please.

MAN: No. Them groceries, two glasses in the house – This wife of yours?

JPW: Questions, if you have any, on the foregoing, please –

MAN: You have a very strange life of it here, Mr King –

JPW: Otherwise, please allow me to continue.

MAN: Are you separated, Mr King?

JPW: Questions on the subject to hand, please.

MAN: Divorced?

JPW: Well, there goes our session.

MAN: There's something wrong somewhere.

JPW: Thank you, that will be all for today.

MAN: No.

JPW: Yes. I am conducting things here.

MAN (*smiling, assessing*): Hah? (*Then he laughs.*)

JPW (*bluffing*): Or – and I am loathed to suggest it – because you have indicated a dissatisfaction with my mode of procedure, you would rather perhaps we discontinued the whole thing entirely –

MAN: No –

JPW: Yes – and had a refund of your money? . . . Yes?

MAN (*considers, then calls* JPW's *bluff*): Yes.

JPW: I mean to say.

MAN: I suppose it'll have to be a refund. You owe me sixty-five pounds.

JPW: . . . Well, a refund is not going to be entirely possible.

MAN: You owe me sixty-five quid.

JPW: I owe you –

MAN: Three sessions –

JPW: No, I don't!

MAN: The first ten, the second –

JPW: The first session, fifteen! Since you are not completing the course.

MAN: Okay. The first fifteen, the second ten, third ten –

JPW: Twenty!

MAN: That's thirty-five pounds –

JPW: Twenty, Saturday, double time! –

MAN: Which leaves sixty-five outstanding.

JPW: Hold, sir, please! Third, today, twenty.

MAN: You're charging me double for today?

JPW: Look at the time! Forty-five pounds. You gave me: hundred, which leaves fifty-five, not sixty-five.

MAN: We agreed –

JPW: A round figure.

MAN: Yes, the hundred that I gave you yesterday.

JPW: Yes. Which leaves –

MAN: On top of that I gave you fifteen on the first day, I gave you a total of a hundred and fifteen. Look, I'm not interested in the money.

JPW: Nor I.

MAN: Yes.

JPW: No. (*Nor I*)

MAN: What?

JPW: I agree.

MAN: So do I.

JPW: I think we should continue too.

MAN: So do I. But.

JPW: What?

MAN: . . . But. Forty-five from a hundred and fifteen, you calculate it.

JPW: That is correct.

MAN: You owe me seventy pounds! Not sixty-five or fifty-five!

JPW (*offering money*): Your name will be included in the draw next week for the rest of it.

MAN (*refusing money*): Not interested in the money . . . So what do we do?

JPW: Well, I don't know, Benimillo.

MAN: Well. (*Going to door. Bluffing about leaving.*) Do we continue tomorrow? It's up to you.

JPW: You don't have to go right now. Do you? I mean to say, Saturday – I'm flexible. And we were approaching certain disturbing areas there and frankly, a crying shame to cut off when we are on the point of some possibly – nitty-gritty. Hmm?

MAN *nods solemnly.*

Have a little drink and we'll take five.

MAN: Well, a little one.

JPW: There. Good luck!

MAN: Cheers!

JPW: Start, stop, cue in, cue out, repeat buttons, nice machine. (*He catches* MAN *smiling in satisfaction to himself.*) You are a bit of a bastard, Benimillo.

MAN (*chuckling*): You're not so bad yourself.

They laugh: more drinks: eyes on the record-player: then laughing again and silent again, their eyes on the machine (a reminder of what has to be achieved).

MAN: Was there anything at all in that talk of yours?

JPW: Frankly, I cannot remember a word of it. I think there was.

Laughter. They are getting quite drunk. Drinking through the following.

MAN: Yeh know, normally, I'd've thought of you as a parasite. But no. And there's a fighter in you somewhere. And similarities somewhere between us. Good luck!

JPW: I don't think so. Good luck.

MAN: No. There's something – some ideals in you too.

JPW: Well, maybe a similarity. You were a great one for the main chance, I was a carnal opportunist. But one of them brought me to my knees.

MAN: Not for sex?

JPW: No, not in this case. Well, at the start at any rate. Actually, I have found sex a disappointing answer to the riddle of life.

MAN: I respect you for that.

JPW: On moral grounds? Gosh, you are laughing again. We must write this down. (*As if writing.*) Bitterness leads to false gaiety. There!

MAN: You're not married. Just as there's no house, sylvan dwelling, there's no wife.

JPW: I am not queer.

MAN: I know. But you're not married! – You're not married! – Never were! – Now!

JPW: Isn't your triumph in this discovery excessive?

MAN: Now! I enjoy our sessions.

JPW: So do I!

MAN: Cocoa and silver salvers! Fiction, fantasy.

JPW: I am entitled to a little fantasy too.

MAN: And roses round the door.

JPW: Clematis.

MAN: Clematis. Now for yeh!

JPW: But there is a woman.

MAN: . . . That brought yeh to your knees? . . . Not the lady, that nice big woman that was here?

JPW (*silently*): No.

MAN: Yeh?

JPW: You want to talk about me?

MAN: It's only fair.

JPW: You are not writing a book, Benimillo? Gosh, you are laughing again.

MAN: She's a beauty? Helen . . . Wha'?

JPW: Yes. Beauty: a shy, simple, comely, virtuous, sheltered, married maiden . . . The resolution to all my problems, whatever they are.

MAN: Someone to darn your socks.

JPW: Yes. That would be an achievement.

MAN: Always the married ones?

JPW: No. I'm unlucky. The discovery that she was already married deterred me but, after six months of it, I could not stop myself and I wrote to her my confession of love. Such a thing to her madonna face was out of the question.

MAN: Yeh?

JPW: She requested an interview which I granted in a car park. The sheltered married maiden's reply to my confession, 'Why do men always take me by surprise?' I was struck dumb: her husband apart, I was not the first to notice her beguiling innocence and domestic potential. When I recovered from the shock, I realised I was serious about her. And began a series of written and oral entreaties which were to continue for a number of years.

MAN: How many?

JPW: Four. All to no avail . . . The thing was getting out of hand . . . This simple married maiden was proving to be a peculiar combination of flirtatious and seductive behaviour which, having aroused me, instantly turned to resistance and rejection. She was now my sole goal in life, and I neglected all else. Would you believe, even a call to Mama's deathbed. I was otherwise engaged.

His laughter, punctuating this story, is pitiful and sounds more like crying.

MAN: Two children.

JPW (*nods*): I made a vow: I would celibate myself, keep myself pure for her. And I added the further precaution of becoming vegetarian, and eating only health foods. And further, I swore that if she should come to bed with me for one short hour and sweet, I would repay her by ending my life there and then.

MAN: You told her that?

JPW: Why not? A present of a locket was not going to be much use in this case. . . . One short sweet hour to allow my wounds to bleed . . . And I would say to her in the car park, how remarkable, you and I alive in Time at the same time. And she would say, but why me? What fate is following me that wreaks havoc in men's hearts, they lose all care for themselves, their jobs, their everything.

MAN: She was having a great time.

JPW: She –

MAN: Oh she was leading you a merry dance.

JPW: No.

MAN: Oh, I know Irishwomen.

JPW: No.

MAN: She was making a right fool of you.

JPW: Benimillo! (*Indicating the door.*)

MAN: And she still is.

JPW: I will not have it. Not from you. You are a very bitter and twisted little man, and I'll thank you to keep your opinions to yourself.

MAN: Okay. Yeh?

JPW: She was very upset.

MAN: You said it brought you to your knees.

JPW: Did I? Well, it is not finished yet. She phones me every single day. It brought the car to a standstill. After a number of final meetings she requested a final meeting. She wanted to tell me that I was a remarkable man and goodbye. So we met. A hurried

meeting. She had even forgotten to take her apron off which I glimpsed beneath her overcoat and which tugged strangely at my heart strings. She said you are a remarkable man and goodbye. She said do not regret it, but you must, you *must,* forget me.

MAN: Regret what?

JPW: You do not understand.

MAN: Don't regret what, you done nothing.

JPW: Benimillo! We were having an affair with the Gods! And despite all the agony I felt a wonder . . . yes, wonder . . . that I should be capable of such sustained intensity about someone and about something for a change . . . Do not regret it, she said, but you must forget me. And though we can never meet again, I shall feel energised at every recurrence of your memory. Happiness and beauty are not meant to mate.

MAN: And that was it?

JPW: I drove away. The familiar companion, a rectangle of pain here. (*Chest to stomach.*) Barely allowing me breath. How could I go on? How to give, yes, such longing, expression. I said shall I stop the car right here in the middle of the street and let whosoever that wishes come along and carry me away to whosoever-whatsoever-wheresoever it wills. So I stopped the car. I did not realise that at this stage I had arrived at the centre of an intersection and that all four streets, each bearing two miles of rush-hour evening traffic converged on me. My broken heart stopped the city. I really do not know how they unravelled it all, nor indeed how long it took them, but by the time the police got to me I was bored by it all! The police thought I was simply a bad driver and I put on my rabbit face. One of them switched on the ignition, three more behind were pushing and telling me to go and get myself – Which I did. Peculiarly enough with a lady in a supermarket. Thus ending four years of celibacy.

MAN: Aw, they're strange people, women. You can forget her.

JPW: Well, we shall finish *our* little job first, then we shall see. (*He switches on the record-player. Gigli singing 'Toselli's Serenade'.*)

MAN: Her name was Ida. (*His gestures, drunkenness becoming operatic.*)

JPW (*turns down volume a little*): Hmm?

MAN: Her name was Ida. She had a grand, a lovely speaking voice, and I felt drawn to her without ever having clapped an eye on her.

JPW: She was a radio announcer.

MAN: Wha'? No! She was a telephonist. I'd never dare go near such a beauty, but, after all, it was on the phone, and I asked her would she like to go for a little walk. The simple way she said yes (gave me a great feeling). I'd never took a girl out before but I walked happy-as-larry, bliss, Mr King, at her side. Looking at the fountains, the monuments, the – wha'?

JPW has started muttering.

JPW: Macerata? Recanati?

MAN: No! Later! Rome! The beggars begging, the English ladies reading poetry, and the lovely little peasant girls that worked as artists' models waiting to be choosed. Wha'?

JPW: Dante? – The poetry – Nothing – You married Ida?

MAN: No! I had to go 'way. But when I come back I rang the exchange. She didn't work there anymore. 'She's been behaving very strange lately' one of the other telephone girls told me.

JPW: Indiscreet remark from a colleague.

MAN: Wha'?

JPW: Go on.

MAN: I ran to her house.

JPW: Dead!

MAN: No! 'You go 'way' her, mother said. Please, I said let me see her. Ida was in hospital.

JPW: Close.

MAN: She had a nervous breakdown. O-o-o!

JPW: A sore thing.

MAN: I ran to the hospital and put the little bunch of flowers on her bed and waited for her to laugh or to cry or to throw open her arms. But she only turned her head away. Her voice – it didn't sound like a voice at all: tired, faint, yeh know, distant. Don't you understand, she said, it's no use.

JPW: Whatever could she mean?

MAN: I fought them, she said. Them? Her mother and father. I held out for ages, she said, but they said it'd killed them. So I gave in. Then I started fainting all the time, she said, now I'm getting better, but I've promised them.

JPW: 'Promised them what?' (*Mimicking Irish Man.*)

MAN: Never to see you again.

JPW: 'But why?'!

MAN: 'But why?' Oh, nothing, she said. You're poor, she said, they say I might as well marry a beggar, they say you'll end up singing in the streets.

JPW: Aah!

MAN: But, Ida! Don't insist, she said, it's no use. You see, I don't love you no more. I couldn't believe it! I rushed from that room, boy. I never saw Ida again.

JPW: What do you think of whore-houses, Benimillo? . . . I could recommend a good one. People there dress up as bishops and things.

MAN: But don't yeh see: the similarities between your story and mine?

JPW: My story is about a real live living person, your story is bullshit. What are you laughing at? (*Beginning to laugh also.*) What are you laughing at?

MAN: One short sweet hour with her, you said, and you'd give your life: I'd give my life for one short sweet hour to be able to sing like that.

JPW (*privately, not convinced*): Would you?

MAN (*going out unsteadily*): One short sweet hour. (*Off.*) One short sweet hour.

JPW Alone.

Evening light has set in during the above, now further deepening to night light. Gigli – muted – singing 'Cielo E

Mar' timed to conclude with end of the scene.

JPW: You see, Benimillo, God created the world in order to create himself. Us. We are God. But that neatly done, God started making those obscure and enigmatic statements. Indeed his son did a lot of rather the same thing. The Last Supper, for instance: the wine, the conversation, *Jewish* wine being passed around. (*He rises unsteadily.*) Christ standing up, 'In a little while you will see me, in a little while you will not see me.' They must have thought the man was drunk. But he had learned the lingo from his father. God taking his stroll in the Garden, as we were told, and passing by innocent Adam, he would nod, and say (*He nods and winks.*) 'I am who am.' And that was fine until one day, Adam, rather in the manner of Newton, was sitting under a tree and an apple fell on his head jolting him into thought. 'Whatever can he mean,' said Adam, 'I am who am?' And he waited until the next time God came strolling by, and he said, 'excuse me' – or whatever they said in those days. I must find out. And he put the question to God. But God said, 'Out out!' 'I only asked!' said Adam. But God said, 'Out!' And naturally, after such rude, abrupt and despotic eviction, the wind was taken out of Adam's intellectual sails: not surprising that he was not up to pursuing the matter. Which is a pity. Because the startling thing, God had got it wrong. Because what does it mean, I am who am? It means, this is me and that's that. This is me and I am stuck with it. You see? Limiting. What God should have been saying, of course, was I am who may be. Which is a different thing, which makes sense – both for us and for God – which means I am the possible, or, if you prefer, I am the impossible. Yes, it is all crystal clear. We understand our existential guilt, our definition of ourselves is right from the start – I am who may be – and, meanwhile, our paradoxical key, despair, is rising, rising in our pool to total despair. That state achieved, two choices. One, okay, I give in, I wait for the next world. Two, what have I to lose and I take

the leap, the plunge into the abyss of darkness to achieve that state of primordial being, not in any muddled theocentric sense, but as the point of origin in the *here-and-now* where anything becomes possible. Now you follow! (*He laughs in celebration.*) And I have three more days to do it!

Possibly during some point in this the silhouette of MONA *arriving outside. She knocks, calls his name 'Jimmy'. He ignores her – she goes away. He turns up the volume: 'Cielo E Mar', ending Act Two triumphantly, and, possibly, a beat later, as lights come up in the auditorium, the trio from 'Attila'.*

Scene Five

The quartet from Rigoletto *introduces and continues into this Scene.*

JPW *dishevelled and exasperated;* MAN *also dishevelled – unusual for him – bewildered and carrying a hang-over. The office door is open and continues so through the Scene.*

JPW *has locked himself in the washroom:* MAN *is banging on the washroom door.*

MAN: She's gone, gone, gone, left me!

JPW (*off*): I don't care, I don't care, I don't care!

MAN: I called last night, you wouldn't let me in! I know you were in!

JPW: I was meditating!

MAN: She took my son!

JPW *comes out angrily, clad in a blanket.*

JPW: I don't care! Our fourth meeting, two to go, and frankly you are confusing and boring the arse off me. (*Striding to the machine.*) Jesus, that machine! (*Switches it off.*) I went to bed last night with the repeat button switched on, I woke up this morning and it was still playing. Heaven knows what it has done to my brain! And speaking of singing, listen – (*Operating a button to the end of the quartet.*) Galli Curci, she is quite the best thing on it. (*He listens to the final notes. He switches off the record-player.*) Supernal last note.

MAN: My wife has left me!

JPW: I don't care! (*He goes to bed.*)

MAN: She took my son!

JPW: I don't care!

MAN: Will you listen to me!

JPW: She will have returned home before you this afternoon.

MAN: I don't want her back!

JPW: So all is well.

MAN: I'll never forgive her. She says she's afraid I'll hurt the child. I never hurt her! So how can she say such a thing? I thought I was very well when I left here yesterday.

JPW: You were drunk.

MAN: I thought I was very well last night but it took me by surprise again.

JPW: Ben-i-millo!

MAN: I started shouting. My son, crying, down the stairs, 'She's only trying to help'. She's only trying to help! It was brave of him, brave little boy, yes, but she's only trying to help. She'd went upstairs, haggard face, up to bed, only trying to help me? And I was feeling very well.

JPW: You were drunk.

MAN: Wha'? I *roared* at the child. Obscenities. Brave little boy. But now she'd got her suitcase. And took him with her. His face to the back windscreen, driving away, tears running down his face, waving bye-bye, bye-bye, like a baby . . . and I just stood there, the lights driving away, don't go, don't go . . .

JPW: You are a terrible drinker. You're a *terrible* drinker!

MAN: Wha'? . . . I told you I was!

JPW: Terrible. (*He gets up.*)

MAN: It's not my problem?

JPW (*sharing the last of a bottle with him*): Well, it is a problem this morning.

MAN: And I left my Gigli record here with you.

JPW: Here, the last hair of the dog.

MAN (*takes glass unconsciously*): I

wouldn't hurt my child.

JPW: Now it is Sunday morning and you arrived – what?, three hours early! – and great lapsed churchgoing people that we are, half of this city is still sensibly in its bed. But you have got me up and, double-time or not, I want something more for my endeavours, so . . . Yes! Sex, if you please.

MAN: I don't think I would hurt my son. Or her.

JPW: I'll give you a kick-off then. My first sexual encounter was in mixed-infants.

MAN: My wife –

JPW: Only matters sexual now or I-shall-not-listen!

A silent contest of wills. JPW, *determinedly, swivels his chair about, his back to* MAN.

MAN: Maisie Kennedy.

JPW: Yes?

MAN: She took me to the end of our garden where the potatoes were.

JPW: Yes?

MAN: She, well then, sort of, took me down on top of her, so that we become hid between the drills, and she kept putting sweets into my mouth while she was trying to get my . . .

JPW: You're doing fine.

MAN: Trying to get my – mickey into her.

JPW: Vagina. Yes? (*He goes back to bed.*)

MAN: I enjoyed the sweets, but my mickey was too young to repay her treat.

JPW: Very good – you see? – You are quite normal

MAN: Sex has nothing to do with it!

JPW: Don't stop now – let it all come out – Your first time, what was that like?

MAN: I was twenty-two.

JPW: I was twenty-three, clumsy affair – Sorry.

MAN: I got very excited and I almost ran, hurrying home to tell Danny.

Danny was next in age to me, I was the youngest and I think he was always a bit embarrassed by my – innocence, I think. He was asleep, but I was proud of myself and I wanted to tell him so that he'd see I wasn't a fool. And I woke him up and told him I'd – had it. And he just rolled over and said, 'how many times' and went back to sleep. . . . You see, Danny. (There's a story) . . . You see, my eldest brother had singled out Danny as the one to be put through school, educated. But I don't think school suited our Danny. But I don't think my eldest brother wanted to admit this. But my father, sick and then dying, and my eldest brother had took over, and he became a sort of tyrant.

JPW: That would be Abramo?

MAN: Mick. Mick frightened us all. Shouting, kicking his bike. Kicking the doors, shouting. My mother thought the world of him. He used to parade his learning too. 'Can anyone tell me what was St Bernadette's second name?' 'Soubrou', or whatever it was. Imagine, he used to give Danny tests. In arithmetic, I suppose. And I'd be sitting quietly, hoping, praying, that Danny, locked upstairs in that room, would pass Mick's examination paper . . . And Danny was always trying to teach me – cunning, I think. Street sense. He used to tell me never trust anyone, and everything is based on hate. He used to tell me that when I got big, if I was ever in a fight with Mick, to watch out, that Mick would use a poker. I suppose he knew he'd never be able for Mick. Unless he shot him, or knifed him. But we didn't do things that way . . . I wanted to be a priest. I was crazy, I was thirteen. But some notion in my head about – dedicating? – my life to others. But Mick, in consultation with my mother – and rightly so – said wait a couple of years. And one day – and the couple of years weren't up – and Mick was in a black mood. And he'd beaten Danny that day too for something or other, and I had went outside. Oh, just outside, sitting on the patch of grass. And. There's only two flowers for children from my kind of background. The daisy and the . . . the yellow one.

JPW: Primrose.

MAN: The primrose too – the buttercup. Oh, just sitting there, picking them off the grass. And Mick come out. What about the priesthood, he said. I'd changed my mind but I didn't tell him. I said – I stood up. The couple of years isn't up, I said. But he knew I'd changed my mind and he said, you're stupid, and he flattened me. I knew what he was at, I was learning. That day the priesthood would've gave the family a bit of status. But, unfortunately for the family, that day I'd changed my mind. . . . Oh yes, the flowers. (*A tremulous sigh.*) Ah. I still had this, little, bunch of flowers. In my hand. I don't think I gave a fuck about the flowers. A few – daisies, and the – the yellow ones. But Danny – he was eighteen! – and he was inside, crying. And it was the only thing I could think of. (*He is only just managing to hold back his tears.*) And. And. I took the fuckin' flowers to our Danny . . . wherever he is now . . . and, I said, which do you think is nicest? The most beautiful, yeh know? And Danny said 'Nicest?', like a knife. 'Nicest? Are you stupid? What use is nicest?' Of what use is beauty, Mr King.

JPW (*gently*): Two million pounds later, Benimillo?

MAN: Actually, a little more.

JPW: James, Jimmy.

MAN: But I've strayed from your subject, Mr King.

JPW: That's okay. Would you like a cup of tea?

MAN (*nods 'Yes' then*): In assets. I never keep much cash.

JPW: And I bet you had no breakfast. Tck! You need your food (*He has got up again and put on his trousers.*)

MAN: I think I should go home. (*But he does not move.*) Do you have brothers and sisters?

JPW: No. Just me.

MAN: And you never went back to see your mother before she died?

JPW: Oh, Mama's not dead. She tried to take her life when Father died. She loved him. Though their worlds were worlds apart. But they brought her back. Or she came back. Extraordinary, because she was always rather delicate. And apparently she was calling my name. Oh, we had a deal – Father and I – which I kept. He promised he would give me five hundred pounds if I did not take a drink until I was twenty-five.

MAN: Why didn't you go back since?

JPW: Not with tail between my legs, Benimillo. What did your brother do, the authoritative one, Mick?

MAN: Oh, something the equivalent of shovelling shit. (*Laughs harshly, vindictively.*) And it took him forty years to become a clerk!

JPW: Let me clear some of these things out of the way. A frustrated young man –

MAN: He wasn't a young man, he was in his thir- (*Thirties*). He wasn't a young man.

JPW: Do you take sugar? Mick was hardly twenty at the time. There was a fattening bag of 'comelackt shoekree erin' (*Comhlucht Siúicre Éireann, sugar*) about the place at one point.

MAN: I don't feel inclined to forgive anyone . . . And I'll never forgive her for last night.

He continues motionless through the following, all the time faced at the open doorway. JPW still preparing tea.

JPW: Kettle? (*Which is in his hand.*) That's the kettle. Water? (*Checks kettle.*) That's water. (*He plugs in kettle and sits watching it.*) I used to watch my father too, secretly. Pottering with one of the gardeners. Straight back, head bowed, looking at his flowers and vegetables as if he was puzzled by them. I wanted to take his hand. But fathers, you know?, formal, straight backs, frowning, unsure of themselves. I think they feel a little spare, and that is a pity.

MAN: Did he pay up? Before he died.

JPW: Oh yes, always kept his word. I bought my first car with that five hundred. Yes, I think he loved her. And me. And Mama, though I was

otherwise engaged when she was calling, would know that I loved her too. Now to wash my best china. (*He has gone to washroom with two mugs.*)

MAN: Sum up?

JPW (*off*): What?

MAN (*beginnings of a roar*): Sum up!

JPW (*off*): Oh! I think you are a basso!

MAN (*hisses at doorway*): I hate! I f-f-f-f . . .

His hand clutching something in his pocket. A few whimpers escape . . . fixed, rooted, in his position, he starts to shout, savage, inarticulate roars of impotent hatred at the doorway . . . developing into sobs which he cannot stop. Terrible dry sobbing, and rhythmic, as if from the bowels of the earth. (The 'performance' an atonal aria?)

JPW emerging wide-eyed from the washroom. The sobbing continuing.

JPW: Yes . . . yes . . . That's it, Benimillo . . . That is what it is like . . . Let it come out . . . Take my hand . . . if you so wish to . . . We all love you, Benimillo . . . Very good . . . That is very good . . .

MAN (*sobs subsiding into tears*): Sorry.

JPW: I know.

MAN: I'm sorry.

JPW: I know.

MAN: I'm sorry.

JPW: I know . . . And you are so tired . . . I know.

MAN: To sing? To sing?

JPW: I know. We'll do it.

MAN: To sing. (*The sobbing finished, tears and laughter.*)

JPW: Goodness gracious! . . . What! . . . Good heavens! I have never heard such crying! What? Good grief! Dear me! My word! That was some – what! And the kettle is boiling! (*Tending to kettle, making tea.*) And we shall have a little music in a moment. Actually, my worst sexual experience was not my first one, or second, or third. One of those half-virgins. A simple soul, God bless her. But she thought we were destined for the altar and, consequently, she was covering herself against the possibility of a post-marital attack. Because she had not been completely virgo intacta for me, her future husband. The stable-boy had got in there when she was only fourteen she told me. 'I think he half done me', she said, 'but Daddy caught him.' Caught him where, I wonder? Well, my girl, I said, now you can feel secure at last in the fact that you have just been fully done. And I congratulated her on having received from my good self the official stamp and approval of A-one fulfilling sexual intercourse. Her simple face fell. Was that what that was, she said. The startling thing, I was thirty-one years of age at the time. Left me with a few complexes for a while, I can tell you. Now, a little music. (*He switches on the machine.*) And the tea. Benimillo? . . . Benimillo?

MAN *is asleep on the bed. Gigli singing 'Agnus Dei'. JPW picks up MAN's hat which is on the floor, gets an idea, hides the hat. JPW sitting reading, with his tea . . . lights fading to evening light. JPW switches on his reading lamp . . . engrossed in book.*

MAN *waking up: a certain disgust at discovering himself in the surroundings, and in JPW's bed, and the music playing. The end of the 'Agnus Dei' cross-fading into 'Cangia Cangia Tu Voglie' by Fasola.*

JPW: Awake at last. You needed that sleep . . . Hmm?

MAN *asks silently for permission to wash his hands in the washroom. He exits to washroom.*

Sum up? Or shall I make some fresh tea? . . . The truth is, we have become fast friends . . . What?

Church clock chiming eight. MAN enters. A brief look about for his hat.

Tomorrow we start transcending a few things, Tuesday you sing . . . Your record! You'll need it tonight.

MAN *has gone out door.*

See you tomorrow! . . . Twelve o'clock.

But MAN is gone. The four walls, the

vodka bottle empty, JPW considers the phone, rejects it . . . restless . . . produces MAN's hat . . . considering going out . . . considers phone again. Makes usual adjustment to connection box, then changes his mind about making phone call (but forgets to make re-adjustment to the connection box). He gets his jacket and a tie (in preparation for the morning). He puts on MAN's hat and sits, tie dangling unconsciously from his hand . . . Gigli sings on, 'Cangia, Cangia, Tu Voglie' to its conclusion.

Scene Six

Office empty, record-player switched off, church clock chiming twelve. JPW comes hurrying in. He has added the old tie to effect a less casual dress and he is wearing MAN's hat. He is pleased he has got back to his office in time and is arranging himself in anticipation of MAN's call. He switches on the record-player. Various paper bags from his pockets, a quarter bottle of vodka . . . waiting . . . loosens his tie . . . has a swig of vodka . . . Looking out the door, the window . . .

JPW: Benimillo . . . Benimillo . . .

Gigli singing 'Puisqu'on Ne Peut Pas Flechir'. Lights fading. Another swig of vodka.

Scene Seven

MAN *has come into office. JPW alseep on the bed.*

MAN: Mr King! Mr King!

JPW: What?

MAN: Mr King!

JPW: Who is that?

MAN: I'd like to have a word with you.

JPW: What time is it?

MAN: Mr King?

JPW: Come in.

MAN: I'm in! (*He switches off the machine.*)

JPW (*fully awake*): Benimillo! Come in,

my friend, sit down!

MAN: I'll stand if you don't mind.

JPW: Benimillo!

MAN: Mr King –

JPW: Have I got stories for you! Have I got the goodies for you!

MAN: Mr King!

JPW: You never let me get a word in edgeways!

MAN: Mr King, this has gone on too long. But before I go into that, I'd like to say something about yesterday.

JPW: What day is today?

MAN: You may think you can read my mind, well, you can't.

JPW: What?

MAN: Better men have tried and failed. Bigger men and better games than this. Or trying to influence me with trickster stuff, hypnosis and the likes, I suppose. Well, you can't. I'd lose you and find you. I know what you've been up to.

JPW: Oh yesterday! I shouldn't feel embarrassed about yesterday.

MAN: I'm not – Do I look embarrassed to you?

JPW: Emotional incontinence. People break down here all the time, my friend.

MAN: Who broke down?

JPW: Curley Wee then perhaps?

MAN: Oh yes, cheap cracks, jokes –

JPW: I thought we had a terriffic day yesterday!

MAN: Listen, I'd just like you to know for one thing, boy, that I had a very happy childhood. You'd like to suggest otherwise, but I'm up to you. Deprived of my father, yes, but my mother, my mother, the Lord have mercy on her, *liked* my father very much, and I often seen her crying. Often, she'd tell me, tears in her eyes, how my father was good to his mother when his mother was old and decrepit, tears in her eyes, that my father slept in the same room – the same bed! – as his mother to nurse and look after her every need. Tears in my mother's eyes telling me that, boy. And Mick – Mick! – often he'd give me

a penny of a Friday to go out and buy a copy-book for myself. Out of his six shilling pay-packet, and the rest to my mother. Oh, but, five hundred pounds to buy a motor car! And crashed it, I suppose! – Your breed would laugh at a six shilling pay-packet, let alone a penny! I just thought I'd let you know. A very happy childhood.

JPW: That's good. You are already on to the next stage, transcending, celebrating the past. (*Offering him a drink.*)

MAN: Celebrating the – No, I don't want your drink, then on to dirty stories and then pumping me for more information. And Mick – Mick! – Mick was a good singer – when he wanted to. 'The Snowy-breasted Pearl', boy. Thought I'd let you know.

JPW: Did your wife return?

MAN: What! Is that any business of yours? Wasting my time and my money as if it grew on the trees. I should have done it myself like I always done. But what a fool, I came to you. Why are you smiling?

JPW: I'm not. (*But he is inclined to laugh.*)

MAN: Mr King – Mr King! You done nothing. Now I think I deserve something more for my time and money. Before I go, is-there-anything-you-can-tell-me? Why are you laughing? . . . You're laughing because you don't know or there's something funny?

JPW: I thought you weren't going to show up!

MAN: That's all you can say?

JPW: Well, has anyone told you you look twenty years younger since you started coming to me?

MAN: They haven't. Anything else?

JPW: Well, you do.

MAN: And that's it? Pathetic. I told you at the start I have little or no time for psychiatrists, now I have none whatsoever for quacks. And yes, my wife is back. And yes, I made my first attempt for months to make conversation with her at lunchtime. I

told her I was simply bored to
distraction: she took it as a reflection
on herself and left the room in tears.
You're not able to explain that either,
I suppose? I left her there – why
wouldn't I? – and drove out into the
country for myself, the first time in
months, beautiful nature all around
me, fine sites for development. Will I
build a thousand more? No. I've made
up my mind on that one. There's more
to life than working myself to death.
Or wheeling and dealing with that
criminal band of would-be present-day
little pigmy Napoleons we've got at the
top. Let them have the profit. I need a
breath of fresh air. Stopped the car to
get out and my only other last hat blew
away – (*Sees his hat.*) – Jesus, there's
the other one! Well, fuck the fuckin'
hats! (*He throws his hat from him.*)

JPW: Bis! Bis!

MAN: What? Hah?

JPW: I did not expect it until tomorrow,
but not quite Gigli yet.

MAN: Look, Mr King, be warned. I
could have you locked up, like that,
one telephone call. But why go
throwing good money after bad. And it
was my own fault. I just can't get over
what possessed me to come into a
place like this, when I can cure myself
like I did last time.

JPW: Last time?

MAN: *And* the time before that!

JPW: How often do you get depressed?
Unhappy.

MAN: Not that it's any of your business,
but smart man that you think you are,
and because I can do what you can't,
I'll tell you. Once every year or two.
Last time I just went away and hid in a
corner – you learn a lot from animals –
like a dog in a corner, you couldn't
prise me out of it, and stayed there
licking my wounds till I cured myself.

JPW: You should have told me.

MAN (*laughs at him*): The time before,
boy, I went into your territory,
debauchery, Mr King: got a dose of the
clap in the course of the treatment, but
I cured myself.

JPW: And the next time?

MAN: I'm looking forward to it already.

JPW: You should have told me.

MAN: About what?

JPW: The pattern!

MAN: That would have made all the
difference, would it?

JPW: You told me you wanted *to sing.*

MAN: I did. The other times I wanted to
do other things.

JPW: Tap-dancing?

MAN *laughs at him*

And I told someone this morning that
this was a once-off do-or-die aspiration,
that there was no pattern – Because
that is what you told me! – and how
astonishing it would be to achieve it.

MAN: And so much for your
confidentiality. Hah?

JPW: I'd be wary of the next one,
Benimillo.

MAN: I mut remember that. Charlatan,
quack, parasite! And, yeh know,
there's a stink in this pig-sty: you'd be
better off cleaning it up. Sum up?

JPW: . . . Yes. Last year, ladies,
debauchery and the clap, this year,
grand opera and me. And I done
nothing? (*Producing books from
various places.*) Here, these are yours.
Kierkegaard, you read it, make sense
of it, stolen out of the South Side
Library. Here, Jung, Freud, Otto Rank
Ernest Becker, Stanislav Grof,
anonymous donations to your cause,
courtesy of Eason's, Greene's – Trinity
College! Heidegger, try sitting up all
night with him for jolly company.
What's this? No, you have this one
already, 'Memoirs of Beniamino Gigli'
– Ida treated him badly alright. Wait!
This is your property, you hired me to
procure it and there is not a decent
library or bookshop in Dublin that I
have not shadily visited to get it for
you. I'm summing up, it's my turn, and
it is only fair! Do you know, Benimillo,
how hard it is to get an appointment
with a psychiatrist at short notice? I
managed two this morning. I, as you,
arrived early for one appointment and

saw the Chief himself going into his office. I slipped in after him, wearing your hat, my hand in my pocket – like you do it. The Chief thought he was in for it! I dropped to my knees, my hands in the air, to reassure him. I said I want to sing like Gigli, my father was a cobbler, bis-bis-bis, can you help me? The Chief, in a whisper, 'Just a mo. Excuse.' Luckily I went to the keyhole, he was rounding up his men, and deputising others to prepare a padded cell. They nearly nabbed me. Out the front door, in the back, met by the pursuing posse, out again, three times round the garden, hid in a bush, the berberis family – look at the scratches! Until I figured they had figured I had escaped. But I had to get in there again, an official appointment for a quarter to ten. Could not risk the front door, or the back, so what was there to do! In through the window of the waiting room. Two waiting patients left, cured. Sweated it out behind the 'Beano' until I was called to the third-assistant psychiatrist's office where I – you – Mickeleen O'Loughlin had an appointment. The psychiatrist was a lady, in years just a little over-ripe – but that was the last thing on my mind. I want to sing like Gigli, I was born in Recanati, bis-bis-bis, can you help me? Was I homosexual? I told her about Ida. Was I *sure* I was not homosexual? She had at this stage taken off her not-very-sensible shoes for-a-lady-of-her years under the desk, and was now removing her spectacles to suck them slyly sideways. 'Tell me, Mr O'Loughlin, what do you expect of me?' she said softly. I misinterpreted – I was losing my nerve: I told her I thought she was beautiful. No, she said, did I expect medication, analysis or therapy from her. Could I have a glass of water and an aspirin, please, I said, and while I had her occupied, I was stealing the six sheets that I now needed from her prescription pad. Goodness knows what that aspirin was, I have not been feeling well all day. But I took it – loudly! – demonstrating my great preference above all else for medication. Because we, Benimillo, had been most remiss, neglecting so completely to enlist the power of medication to sing like Gigli, and I set

to pumping her on the subject. Oh, and do you know her fees? Thirty pounds! Hmm? For twenty-five minutes! I thought it was all for free! Cheque or cash? Send the bill, I said. Gave my correct address too – I just could not think fast enough: the surprise that one could make enormous fortunes at this game, plus the further complication, the Chief's voice once more in the hall: he was now calming down his men, and they were nearly back to normal. But I could not risk it: they are most dedicated people, and I did not have the further strength to run if they got excited again. So, thank you, to the good lady, and excuse me, as I slipped out to the rose-garden through *her* window.

MAN: I'm sorry.

JPW: Not at all.

MAN: I'm –

JPW: Not at all!

MAN: I didn't think –

JPW: All part of the service.

MAN: I'll call you tomorrow.

JPW: No tomorrow.

MAN: I didn't mean –

JPW: You did mean! I-have-not-finished! You did mean. And you are quite right. Here, these, also, are for you – (*the small paper bags he returned with*). Sweeties, on forged prescriptions. Insidon, anti-downers, one three times daily will get you to a high C, but do not expect results for ten days. And drink is out with them, negates the effects. For faster results – if you are getting impatient, anxious – Tranxene, take one about two hours before retiring. If you should find that it does not get you through the day singing – where's my topper-up? – Here – Nobrium – Excellent name for this kind of stuff whoever thought it up. Nobrium, a supplement, take one at tea-time if required. What are these? – Here – No, these are for myself: Frisium, to put bounce back into my hair (*He takes some*) – and tranquilize my nerves. And a mild sleeping pill. Sorry, but I really need these, because I have not had a moment's peace or a decent hour's sleep since I clapped eyes on you.

MAN: Jimmy.

JPW: No! You did mean! And you are quite right to walk in here four hours late. It is a pig-sty, I am a charlatan and a quack, and I have *never* achieved *anything* in my life! And stupid, you left out that one. I even learned the baritone role of the duet on that thing – and I am the *tenor!* – thought we might give it a whirl together tomorrow. *I-am-the-tenor!*

MAN: I spoke out of turn.

JPW: And that gun that you have been terrifying me with.

MAN: What gun?

JPW: And I am sure there will be a warrant out for my arrest.

MAN: What gun?

JPW: Your trump card, the final word, that gun in your pocket that you have been threatening to shoot yourself with, or me – I never knew which.

MAN: These? (*He produces a small cylindrical container of pills.*) Mandrax, sleeping pills. (*He dumps them in the wastepaper basket.*)

JPW: . . . Do you think you have *got* me then?

MAN: No.

JPW: Do you think you have won?

MAN: No. No.

JPW: Well, you have not! Have you seen it through?

MAN: I'll call –

JPW: Is this what you call seeing it through?

MAN: I'll call and see you –

JPW: Well, you have not!

MAN: When you have cooled down.

JPW: You have not!

MAN: When you have –

JPW: Rather not. No! . . . No.

MAN *goes out.*

JPW: You have not won, Benimillo. I have not finished.

Absently, he takes a handful of the pills nearest to him and washes them down with vodka. He switches on record-player. Gigli singing 'Tu Che A Dio Spiegasti L'Ali' from Lucia De Lammermoor with bass and chorus. He emits a few pitiful howls in attempt at singing. The telephone rings. He approaches it cautiously, like a man approaching a trap . . . lifts receiver.

. . . Hello? . . . Hello? . . . Who? Helen? . . . Helen! . . . Are you still there? . . . Fine . . . I have been very fine. (*Silently.*) Helen! . . . No, I'm still here. I just cannot, I mean to say – Helen! . . . What? . . . Music. Beniamino Gigli . . . You've heard of him? Really? (*Celebratory laugh.*) Born in Bunratty (or, Killarney) . . . No, I'm laughing because, I mean to say – how are you? . . . What is the matter? . . . Why are you crying? . . . Why are you . . . Pardon? . . . I did not phone you yesterday because . . . I did not phone you the day before because . . . You asked me not to. To promise, not to call you. You – what? . . . (*Shocked.*) I am a what? . . . A what? . . . Dirty – I never made a dirty phone call to you . . . And if I ever call you again you shall . . . Send the police! . . . Hello? . . . Hello? (*He puts down the phone.*) Bloody hell.

He sits there stunned . . . he remembers the Mandrax and is on his hands and knees searching the waste-paper basket for them. MONA arrives.

MONA: Well, lover! Some batteries for your shaver and a present. (*She puts batteries, a pot plant and a bottle of vodka on the desk, and she leaves an overnight bag which she is carrying somewhere. She goes to the record-player.*) What's this? (*She turns down the volume.*)

JPW (*absently*): I am very busy right now, Mona. Bloody hell. (*He finds the container of Mandrax; he is half-frightened of them, then becoming conscious of MONA, and relieved by her presence. He puts the Mandrax in his pocket.*) Mona! You would not believe it, people are crazy! You are the absolutely only normal human being in the world! (*He has come up behind her and circled her waist with his arms. She likes the feeling of his arms around her, but the cloud of her secret sadness is moving aross her face.)* And how is Karen Marie, your god-child?

MONA: What god-child?

JPW (*not listening*): Isn't that interesting?

A wry, sad smile, she is turning away in the direction of the bed, the music cross-fading from whatever is playing to the final section of the sextet from Lucia de Lammermoor to 'Caro Mio Ben', leading into the final scene.

Scene Eight

JPW *and* MONA *dressed as before –* MONA *minus her overcoat and gloves – lying on the bed, something childlike about them, huddled together, eyes on the record-player, listening to the music. Gigli singing 'Caro Mio Ben' followed by* 'Amarilli'.

MONA: . . . That's the fourth – fifth? – time round. You could go away for a year with that thing switched on and it would still be playing when you got back.

JPW: Yeh.

MONA: How many were singing in the last one?

JPW: The Sextet?

MONA: I like that best.

JPW: Yeh.

MONA: How many were singing in it?

JPW: The Sextet? Three.

MONA: What's he singing, what's he saying now?

JPW: You don't have to know, whatever you like.

MONA: Beloved.

JPW: If you like.

MONA: That everything ends.

JPW: Yes. But that, *at least,* we end up friends. At least that.

MONA: That everything ends anyway. And does it matter – does-it-matter! – if it all ends now, a few seconds earlier, for God's sake! . . . Jimmy.

He offers her the bottle of vodka absently. She declines. She looks at her watch.

JPW: That you are breathing, now, this moment . . . alive in Time at the same time as I . . . and that I can only hold my breath at the thought.

MONA: That's nice.

JPW: Beloved.

MONA: Why don't you call me that? . . . There's someone or something wounding you, very deeply, and I can't do a thing about it.

JPW (*a new thought*): No. That is what I *used* to think. (*Offering her the bottle again.*) *You* and I are alive in Time at the same time.

MONA: I'm not meant to. (*Then she changes her mind, a silent 'fuck it' and she takes a swig.*) Why do you put up with it?

JPW: You're not listening to me.

MONA: When life is –

JPW (*celebratory laugh*): Bouncing back! Isn't that interesting? Bother the lot of them.

MONA: When life is short. And *I'm* here. Well – (*About to qualify the last, changes her mind.*) Some bird you want to screw, is it? I'd do that for you in a wheelchair on the fucking moon. The way some of you mope about. I know you think I'm vulgar.

JPW: No. I think you are –

MONA: Well, I am not. Oh fuck it, maybe I am. But all our family is! Brothers, sisters, Mammy, Daddy – ten of us! – you should hear us all together! We're all vulgar! But the way I look at things, if life is, as they say, just a preparation for heaven, then what's the big deal about life about?

JPW: What are you talking about?.

MONA: But if there is no heaven, what's the big deal about heaven about? So, I say, make the most of what's available now, grab what you can.

JPW opens his mouth to speak.

Yes, pleasure too, but I mean even more. All that energy about. Why are people moping? All that energy in the world, to be enjoyed, to kill pain, to give to the children.

JPW: What's wrong?

MONA (*she has another long swig of vodka*): And watch them grow up.

JPW: You are not listening.

MONA: . . . I'm listening to you. Do you know what he's (*Gigli*) saying? A baby. That's what it's all about.

JPW: The farmer's wife. (*He is looking at her intently, seeing her potential.*) And a lot of easy money to be made in farming. I could be a farmer.

MONA *laughs*.

Well, it's possible.

MONA: That's what you said to me in the supermarket, anything is possible.

JPW: We are a very good team, Mona.

MONA: Too late.

JPW: Hmm?

MONA: You wouldn't be able to buy a farm now anyway. Why didn't you invest your money?

JPW: Yes, well, but. I'm glad you're here.

MONA: I know. I feel it for the first time.

JPW: Do you? (*Isn't that interesting?*) What are you looking at your watch for?

MONA: I wasn't. I got a letter from my young sister today. Do you want to hear?

JPW: Yes. Bother the lot of them. (*He switches off the machine.*) And if he comes back for that (*machine*), I'll have it hocked, tell him it was stolen.

MONA: Here's a bit. This is the hospital where she works and there's this young doctor, and he was passing remarks about 'the pips' under Caroline's uniform. All of us are like that too, up here (*small-breasted*). The girls, that is. (*Reading:*) '. . . the pips under my uniform and I said you wouldn't like one of them up your arse as a pile, would you. So the laugh was on him.' I told you! We all talk like that. (*Suddenly grave.*) But you should see our Caroline. She's beautiful.

JPW: Like you.

MONA: 'Daddy made custard two nights ago and, mind you, it was very nice. So he made it again last night. It was like soup, all lumpy, and no one could eat it. So we gave it to the dogs. All the dogs had their feet in the air in the morning'. It's nice to get a letter when you're not expecting it. But I can see them there, all together, with Daddy's custard. Jimmy, I have cancer. I've been going to doctors for another purpose, but life is full of surprises.

JPW: Breast cancer? (*Motionless – and continues so through the following.*)

MONA: Tck, no! You should know that. Glands, lymphs. I wanted to lie beside you for a while. I've been delaying. I've to go in a minute.

JPW: The lymphatic system?

MONA: Yeh. I go in tonight to start the treatment, nip it in the bud. My husband – honestly, that man! – started crying when I told him. Silly c– Sorry – clunt. Oh for God's sake, I said, I'm-Not-Dead-Yet! (*Aside to him:*) Hard to kill a bad thing. Will you send me flowers?

JPW: New cures all the time.

MONA: Yes! – that's what I told him! – Wonder drugs! And, if the worst comes to the worst, as they say – I have to go, Jimmy – I have no regrets. (*A movement to restrain her from getting up, above. Dressing, overcoat, gloves through the following.*) Well, a few. I had a little girl when I was sixteen. They didn't mean to, but now I know they pressurised me. They wanted the father's name. I wouldn't give it. They needed it to have her adopted. I wouldn't give it. Still, they had her adopted some way. Things hadn't gone right, complications, and I was very ill. I only saw her twice. She was so tiny. She's twenty-two now. Somewhere. I've been trying to repeat the deed ever since. I picked you up. And if I had had a child by you, or any of the others, I don't think I would have told you. I'd have been the one you wouldn't have seen for dust. Pregnant into the sunset. But preferably by you. Others weren't so gentle in how they regarded me. But it couldn't be done.

And maybe just as well now. (*Smiles to herself.*) So I invented a modest god-child, in some kind of – fancy? – in the meantime, to keep me going. But, Karen Marie. Yeh. Maybe just as well now. Well, my magician friend. am I forgetting anything? (*An imperative:*) Water that! (*the potted plant*) See yeh.

He nods.

Beloved?

He nods.

I love you.

She leaves. He switches on the record-player, blasting up the volume – Elisabeth Rethberg/Gigli/Pinza singing the trio 'Tu Sol Quest Anima' from Attila. He is now crying, shouting – in various directions.

JPW: I lo –! (*love*) I love! I –! I –! Fuck you! I love! Fu –! fuck you! I love! – I love! Fuck you – fuck you! I love . . .

Now appearing to be finding a stillness, a purpose out of the blaring singing. He gets the container of Mandrax and takes one; does not like the taste and washes it down with a long swig of vodka. A sudden stomach cramp but he recovers quickly.
Silhouette of MAN *arriving, knocking.* JPW *does not hear him.* MAN *entering – his entrance timed with bass solo in the trio from Attila. He is dressed in tuxedo, smoking a cigar, has had a few drinks; beaming. He is unsure about* JPW's *attitude, whether or not it is to be taken as banter. He has a present of a bottle of vodka. His first lines are spoken under the music.* JPW, *in half doubled-up position, continues motionless for some time.*

MAN: Can I come in? I drank you out of house and home the other day. I was a bit shy, hesitating about calling. Can we have a little one together? Will I open this, or – (*He takes the bottle already opened.*) Waste not, want not, and you'll have a little store in for yourself. Ah, the aul' music! (*He switches off the music and puts a drink into* JPW's *hand.*) The intinerants moved on. Oh, d'yeh mind? (*The cigar.*) They moved on, the creatures. It cost me a few bob but – ah, my place wasn't a suitable place at all for

them. Please God they'll find a more suitable site. They have a tough life of it, and it's not their fault. (*He sits.*) Oh, d'yeh mind? Just for a minute. But I was doing my sums going home in the car and it come into my head. Supposing my life depended on it, who would I turn to? I went through mothers, brothers, relations. The wife. It all boils down to the wife for us all in the end. So we're going out for the evening. I left her (down the road), with some friends for a few minutes. Good luck, God bless, cheers! And I couldn't help thinking – Hah-haa, you're a queer one! – strange as the route you took me, you had some kind of hand in leading me to that conclusion.

JPW: It is Tuesday?

MAN: No. What?

JPW: Final session.

MAN (*laughs*): Aw!

JPW: A refund?

MAN (*laughs*): No!

JPW: But the job is not finished.

MAN: I'm fine – thanks in some measure to you.

JPW: But it can be done. To sing. The sound to clothe our emotion and aspiration. And what an achievement.

MAN: The next time, the one you warned me about.

JPW: No, we have tried laughing, and crying, and philosophy.

MAN: You're a case!

JPW: I have boiled it down to two opinions. Have you considered surgery?

MAN: An operation is it?

JPW (*laughing – but quite likely precipitated by a stomach cramp*): You were taking me seriously there. (*Offering to top up his drink.*)

MAN: No – no – no! I don't know how to take you, Mr King.

JPW: And naughty Benimillo, you have a few in you already.

MAN: And by the looks of you, you've had more than your share. I'd a drop of champagne. Champagne is light, d'yeh know. Was I your first client?

JPW (*absently; looking out window or door*): No. There was one other. It's pretty bad out there, isn't it?

MAN: Oh, now.

JPW: Ever returning, waking up, lying down, more unhappy.

MAN: You can surprise yourself and find yourself strayed too far from the world alright . . . you're looking very pale.

JPW: So I bring my last option into play. Have you considered magic?

MAN: Mr King –

JPW: You are going to ask me what is magic –

MAN: Mr King, Mr King –

JPW: Jimmy! Jimmy!

MAN: Jimmy. Jimmy. And we are friends. And I'm sorry I upset you today, and I'm sorry I have to rush now, but I called because I was wondering if there was some way I could repay all the trouble you took . . . if there was some way at all?

JPW: It is rest for me to take trouble for a friend.

MAN: That's it, that's –

JPW: Persian proverb.

MAN: That's the kind you are, but reality, face the facts. And I'm not talking a hundred, or two hundred. A couple of grand, to set you up. Yeh did a great job.

JPW: No. Not yet.

MAN: I could stretch it to three.

JPW: I shan't hold you. I know you have to rush – And don't tell me: you are going on a holiday? I knew it. These little ceremonies can be pleasantly tranquillizing. You have taken yourself captive again. But dread still lies nesting. Benimillo.

MAN (*preparing to go*): Well, I'm very grateful to you.

JPW: No, I am grateful to you. I longed to take myself captive too and root myself, but you came in that door, with the audacity of despair, wild with the idea of wanting to soar, and I was the most pitiful of spiritless things.

MAN: Well.

JPW: Leave it to me, Benimillo.

MAN: And I did get the right man for the job.

JPW: Oh, and your machine!

MAN: No, you keep that.

JPW (*logically*): But I shan't require it.

MAN: Since you'll take nothing else. No, a little gift . . . Go home, Jimmy. Forget that – Irish colleen. You are a remarkable man. I know there's kindness in the world, but they'll kill you over here. (*Silently:*) Go home.

He leaves. JPW into action. He locks the door, switches off the record-player, then unplugs it from its power point as a double precaution (and proof). He looks out the window for a moment, then draws the blind. He goes to his desk where he spreads jam on a slice of bread, cuts the bread into squares and decorates each square with a Mandrax pill. Through the following, a red glow, as if emanating from the reading lamp with the red shade, suffuses the room, and the shaft of yellow light from the washroom becoming more intense.

JPW: You are going to ask me what is magic. In a nutshell, the rearrangement and redirection of the orbits and trajectories of dynamatological whirlings, i.e., simply new mind over old matter. This night I'll conjure. If man can bend a spoon with beady steadfast eye, I'll sing like Gigli or I'll die. Checklist. Too many facts in the world. Addiction to those lines arrested. Rationalisations, recognised – yes, you have dallied too long with your destiny – All alibis exhausted, desire for achievement, mind set on goal. Trump card – (*He pops a square of bread and jam with pill on top into his mouth and washes it down with vodka.*) And wait. (*After a moment, he opens his mouth as if to sing. An abortive sound/silence. Another piece of bread and jam with pill on top . . .*) And wait. (*Another abortive sound.*) The soul! Of course! The soul of the singer is the subconscious self. Realistic thinking, honest desire for assistance. (*To*

heaven.) Rather not. You cut your
losses on this little utopia of greed and
carnage some time ago, my not so very
clever friend. (*To the floor:*) Assist
please. In exchange – (*Another square
of bread and jam with pill into his
mouth and washes it down with vodka.*)
And wait, wait, wait . . . and wait . . .
until the silence is pregnant with the
tone urgent to be born. (*Faintly – and
as an echo from a distance – orchestral
introduction for the aria 'Tu Che A Dio
Spiegasti L'Ali'. Whispers;*) What!
Yesss! Thank you. But just a mo.
(*Gestures, cueing out music, takes
another pill, a decision against further
vodka.*) Stops taking alcohol, purity of
potion, contentment in abstinence, care
of personal appearance. Diminishing
fears of unknown future . . .
Resolution fixed in mind for
possibilising it. Increase in control to
achieve it . . . Abyss sighted! All my
wordly goods I leave to nuns. Leeeep!
(*Leap*) Pluh-unnge! (*Plunge*) . . . (*Sigh
of relief.*) Aah! Rebirth of ideals,
return of self-esteem, future known.

*He cues in his imaginary orchestra and
we get the orchestral introduction to 'Tu
Che A Dio Spiegasti L'Ali', and he
sings the aria to its conclusion (Gigli's
voice): triumphant, emotional ending.
He is kneeling on one knee; glow of red
light receding, as to its point of origin
(the small reading lamp) and shaft of
yellow light becoming less intense: lights
back to normal. JPW on the floor, on
hands or knees or whatever, eyes
haunted, pained, hurt, frightened. The
church clock chiming six a.m.*

Mama! Mama! Don't leave me in this
dark.

*Some resilience within pulling himself
up . . . He lets up the blind . . . early
morning light filtering into the room
. . . He looks ghastly . . . he wonders if
he is not dead . . . a single gasp or
grunt to check on this . . . remembers
record-player: checks to find that it is
indeed disconnected from its power
point . . . smile, laugh of achievement
on his face. He puts a few things in an
old leather bag and whatever vodka
remains into his pocket. Is about to
leave, gets an idea. He opens the lower
half of his window, plugs in the record-*
*player, switches it on, presses repeat
button, 'invites' the music towards the
open window, Gigli's 'O Paradiso'.*

Do not mind the pig-sty, Benimillo . . .
mankind still has a delicate ear . . .
that's it . . . that's it . . . sing on
forever . . . that's it.

*He unlocks the door and goes out, a
little unsteady on his feet.*

BAILEGANGAIRE

*The story of Bailegangaire
and how it came by its appellation*

Bailegangaire was first performed by the Druid Theatre Company, Galway, on 5 December 1985 with the following cast:

MOMMO	Siobhán McKenna
MARY	Marie Mullen
DOLLY	Mary McEvoy

Directed by   Garry Hynes
Designed by   Frank Conroy
Lighting by   Roger Frith

Time and place: 1984. The kitchen of a thatched house. The set should be stylized to avoid cliché and to achieve best effect.

Note: 'Notturno' in E Flat by Schubert introduces and closes the play. Mary's poem, which she misquotes, in Act One is 'Silences' by Thomas Hardy.

ACT ONE

Dusk is setting in. The room is a country kitchen in the old style. There are some modern conveniences: a bottle-gas cooker, a radio, electric light – a single pendant. Framed photographs on the walls; brown photographs of uncles, one of a christening party. There is a double bed in the kitchen – it is the warmest room in the house (probably the central room of the traditional three-roomed thatched house). An old woman in the bed, MOMMO, is eating and drinking something out of a mug, occasionally rejecting pieces of food, spitting them on the floor. She is a good mimic. She interrupts her meal–

MOMMO: Scoth caoc! Shkoth!

Driving imagined hens from the house.

Dirty aul' things about the place . . .
And for all they lay!

She is senile.

MARY, *her granddaughter, is seated on a box beside the fire; the top of the box – a painted timber butter box – upholstered. MARY looking at nothing, not even at the fire. She wears a wrap-around apron draped tightly about her spinster frame; bare knees over half wellington boots; hair tight, perhaps in a bun. She is forty-one. A 'private' person; an intelligent, sensitive woman; a trier, but one who is possibly near breaking point. It is lovely when she laughs. She does not react to the above. MOMMO has again interrupted her meal to talk to imagined children at the foot of the bed.*

Let ye be settling now, my fondlings, and I'll be giving ye a nice story tonight when I finish this. For isn't it a good one? An' ye'll be goin' to sleep.

The tips of MARY's *fingers to her forehead and she closes her eyes.*

. . . Oh ho, but he bet (*beat*) them. He bet the best of them . . . Incestuous drunkards and bastards.

The kettle on the gas stove is whistling. MARY rises mechanically to make tea, lay the table. She produces the anomaly of a silver teapot . . . MOMMO now watching MARY and MARY's movements suspiciously.

. . . An' no one will stop me! Tellin' my nice story . . . (*Reverts to herself.*) Yis, how the place called Bochtán – and its *graund* (*grand*) inhabitants – came by its new appellation, Bailegangaire, the place without laughter. Now! . . . Jolter-headed gobshites . . . (*Grandly.*) Ooh! and to be sure, and I often heard it said, it had one time its portion of jollification and mirth. But, I'm thinkin', the breed they wor (*were*) 'twas venom, and the dent of it, was ever the more customary manifestation. The land there so poor – Och hona go gus hah-haa, land! – when 'twasn't bog 'twas stone, and as for the weather? 'twas credited with bein' seven times worse than elsewhere in the kingdom. And so hard they had it, to keep life itself in them, whenever Bochtán was mentioned the old people in their wisdom would add in precaution, go bhfóire Dia orainn, may God protect us. What time is it?

MARY: Seven.

MARY *is now taking off her apron.*

MOMMO: Yis! Shkoth! – an' lock them in.
Och haw, but I'll out-do the fox. I'll take the head of the everyone of them tomorrow. Ooh! and to be sure –

MARY (*quietly*): Mommo?

MOMMO: And I often heard it said –

MARY: Mommo? (*She has removed her apron and in her new image is smiling bravely against an increasing sense of loneliness and demoralisation.*) I have a surprise for you.

MOMMO: Pardon?

MARY (*switches on the light*): Look! (*She holds up an iced cake.*) We never knew your birthday but today is mine and I thought we might share the same birthday together in future.

MOMMO (*eyes now fixed on the pendant light bulb*): The cursèd paraffin.

MARY: Though someone said once – I may be wrong – yours was the first of May, a May child – But look! –

MOMMO: The cursèd paraffin.

MARY: And the candles. And another

(*candle*) here, and you can get out of
bed for a little – if you wish.

MOMMO: Birthday?

MARY: Yes! We'll have a party, the two
of us.

MOMMO: What's birthdays to do with
us?

MARY: By candlelight. (*She lights the
candle on the table.*)

MOMMO: What's your business here?

MARY (*indicating the table*): Isn't that
nice?

MOMMO: Do I know you?

MARY: Mary. (*She bows her head,
momentarily deflated, then smiles
invitingly at* MOMMO *again.*)

MOMMO (*and there is defiance, hatred
in the sound*): Heh heh heh heh.

MARY: Mary. (*And she switches off the
light.*)

MARY *picks up a book en route,
switches on the radio and sits at the
table to have her tea. We get the end of
the news in Irish on the radio, then
Tommy O'Brien's programme of light
classics,* Your Choice and Mine. *The
candlelight, the table neatly laid, the
silver teapot, the simple line of Mary's
dress becomes her, the book beside her,
sipping tea, the grave intelligent face, a
picture of strange elegance.* MOMMO
has been continuing.

MOMMO: Ooh! and to be sure and so as
not to be putting any over-enlargement
on my narrative, the creatures left in it
now can still *smile,* on occasion. And
to be sure, the childre, as is the wont
of all childre in God's kingdom on
earth, are as clever at the laughing as
they are at the crying, until they arrive
at the age of reason. That is well, my
dears. Now to tell my story. Here!
You! Miss! Take this. Did you manage
to poison me! Ha-haa – No – ho-ho.

MARY (*takes a cup of tea to* MOMMO
*and places it on the chair beside the
bed, takes the mug*): And I'll get you a
nice slice of cake to go with the tea.

MOMMO: Pardon?

MARY: And isn't that nice music?

MOMMO: Cake?

MARY: Every Sunday night.

MOMMO: Music?

MARY: Yes. Listen.

MOMMO: . . . An' no one will stop me
tellin' it!

MARY, *suspended in the action of
about to cut the cake, now sits at the
table, lights a cigarette, face impassive,
exhaling smoke.*

MOMMO (*settles herself in the bed for
her story*): Now . . . It was a bad year
for the crops, a good one for
mushrooms, and the contrary and
adverse connection between these two
is always the case. So you can be sure
the people were putting their store in
the poultry and the bonavs (*bonhams*)
and the creamery produce for the great
maragadh mór (*big market*) that is held
every year on the last Saturday before
Christmas in Bailethuama (the town of
Tuam) in the other county. And some
sold well and some sold middlin', and
one couple was in it – strangers, ye
understand – sold not at all. And at
day's business concluded there was
celebration, for some, and fitting
felicitations exchanged, though not of
the usual protraction, for all had an
eye on the cold inclement weather that
boded. So, the people were departing
Bailethuama in the other county in
diverse directions homewards. As were
the people of the place I'm talking
about. And they were only middlin'
satisfied, if at all. The Bochtáns were
never entirely fortunate. An' devil
mend them. An' scald them. No
matter. What time is it? . . . Miss!

MARY: Seven. Eight. (*The tips of her
fingers to her forehead.*)

MOMMO: I'm waiting for someone.
Supa tea.

MARY: It's on the chair beside you.

MOMMO: Oh an' he *will* come yet. (*A
warning to* MARY:) And he has a big
stick.

MARY (*remains seated: she knows from
experience what the outcome of the
conversation is going to be; she does
not lift her eyes*): And time to take
your pills.

MOMMO (*has no intention of taking
them*): The yellow ones?

MARY: Yes.

MOMMO: They're good for me?

MARY: I'll give you a cigarette.

MOMMO: They'll help me sleep?

MARY: Yes.

MOMMO: Heh heh heh heh.

MARY (*to herself*): And I'd like to read, Mommo.

MOMMO: Now there was a decent man at that market and his decent wife the same. Strangers, strangers! Sure they could have come from the south of – Galway! – for all I know. And they had sold not at all. Well, if you call the one basket of pullets' eggs valiant trade. (*She takes a sip of the tea.*) Too hot. No. Their main cargo which consisted of eighteen snow-white geese still lay trussed in the floor of the cart, 'gus bhár ar an mí-ádh sin (*and to make matters worse*) the pitch on an incline of the road was proving an impossibility for the horse to surmount. But he was a decent man, and he took not belt – nor the buckle-end of it as another would – to the noble animal that is the horse. Put it down. (*The last to* MARY *who is standing by having put a little more milk into Mommo's tea.*) No. But spoke only in the gentlest of terms, encouraging the poor beast to try once more against the adversary. 'Try again, Pedlar.' For that was the horse's name. Is that a step?

MARY (*listening*): . . . Dolly was to call last night. (*The sound they have heard – if any – does not materialise further.*) Nobody. She didn't call the night before either.

MOMMO: What's this?

MARY *does not understand.*

Taking down the good cup!

MARY: It tastes nicer out of a –

MOMMO: Mug, a mug! – oh leave it so now! Put it down!

MARY: And nicer to have your pills with.

MOMMO: The yellow ones? – Try again, Pedlar, for-that-was-the-horse's name!

MARY *returns to the table.*

And all the while his decent wife on the grass verge and she cráite (*crestfallen*). And a detail which you may contemplate fondly now but was only further testimonial to the misfortunes of that unhappy couple, each time she went to draw the shawl more tightly round her frailty, the hand peepin' out held three sticks of rock. Now! Yis, gifts for her care, three small waiting grandchildren. Like ye. Isn't it a good one? (*A sip of tea.*) Cold.

MARY (*to herself*): I can't stand it.

But she is up again in a moment to add a little hot water and a little more sugar to the tea.

MOMMO: And she up to the fifty mark!

MARY (*to herself*): And that bitch Dolly.

MOMMO: Or was she maybe more?

MARY: In heat again.

MOMMO: And what was her husband? Decorous efficiency in all he cared to turn his hand to, like all small men. Sure he had topped the sixty!

MARY: Taste that and see if it's alright for you.

MOMMO: But he was unlucky. He was. He was. An' times, maybe, she was unkind to him. (*Childlike.*) Was she?

MARY: No. (*Returning to the table where she sits, her head back on her shoulders, looking up at the ceiling.*)

MOMMO: And how many children had she bore herself?

MARY: Eight?

MOMMO: And what happend to them?

MARY: Nine? Ten?

MOMMO: Hah?

MARY: What happened us all?

MOMMO: Them (*that*) weren't drowned or died they said she drove away.

MARY: Mommo?

MOMMO: Let them say what they like.

MARY: I'm very happy here.

MOMMO: Hmmph!

MARY: I'm Mary.

MOMMO: Oh but she looked after her grandchildren

MARY: Mommo?

MOMMO: And Tom is in Galway. He's afeared of the gander.

MARY: But I'm so . . . (*She leaves it unfinished, she can't find the word.*)

MOMMO: To continue.

MARY: Please stop. (*She rises slowly.*)

MOMMO: Now man and horse, though God knows they tried, could see the icy hill was not for yielding.

MARY: Because I'm so lonely.

She puts on her apron mechanically, then sets to work. Progressively working harder: scrubbing that part of the floor MOMMO has spat upon, clearing away and washing up the crockery, washing clothes that have been soaking in a bucket . . . Later in the play, working, working: sheets to be put soaking in a bucket overnight, a bucket of mash for the hens in the morning, bringing in the turf . . .

MOMMO: So what was there for doing but to retrace the hard-won steps to the butt-end of the road which, as matters would have it, was a fork. One road leading up the incline whence they came, the other to Bochtán. Now that man knew that the road to Bochtán, though of circularity, was another means home. And it looked level enough stretching out into the gathering duskess. And 'deed he knew men from his own village (*who*) had travelled it and got home safe and sound. Still he paused. Oh not through fear, for if he was a man to submit he would've threwn himself into the river years ago. No. But in gentleness, sad the searching eye on the road. And sadder still the same grey eyes were growing in handsomeness as the years went by. She had noted it. But she'd never comment on this becoming aspect of his mien for, strange, it saddened her too. It did. But the two little smiles appearing, one each side of his mouth, before taking a step anywhere. Even when only to go to the back door last thing at night an' call in the old dog to the hearth.

MARY *hears the 'putt-putt' of a motorcycle approaching, stopping outside. She pauses in her work for a moment. Then:*

MARY: Right!

Suggesting she is going to have matters out with DOLLY. DOLLY comes in. Like her name, dolled-up, gaudy rural fashion. She is perhaps carrying a crash-helmet. She is thirty-nine. MOMMO is paused in her own thoughts and does not notice DOLLY's entrance; MARY does not acknowledge it, she has resumed working. DOLLY remains with her back to the front door for some time.

MOMMO: . . . Last thing at night . . . An' then the silence, save the tick of the clock . . . An' why didn't she break it? She knew how to use the weapon of silence. But why didn't he? A woman isn't stick or stone. The gap in the bed, concern for the morrow, how to keep the one foot in front of the other. An' when would it all stop . . . What was the dog's name (*Childlike.*) D'ye know I can't remember.

DOLLY: Mo Dhuine (*The One*).

MOMMO: Shep, was it?

DOLLY: Mo Dhuine.

MOMMO: Shep? Spot? Rover? . . . Mo Dhuine! Mo Dhuine! Now! Mo Dhuine.

DOLLY: Jesus.

MOMMO: He loved Mo Dhuine – Och hona ho gus hah-haa! – An' the bother an' the care on him one time filling the eggshell with the hot ember an' leavin' it there by the door.

DOLLY: Then the root in the arse.

MOMMO: Then the root in the arse to poor Mo Dhuine, the twig 'cross his back, to get along with him an' the mouth burned in him! Oh but it did, *did,* cured him of thievin' the eggs.

DOLLY *switches on the light.*
MOMMO's *eyes to the light bulb.*

DOLLY: What're yeh doin' workin' in the dark?

MOMMO: But they had to get home.

DOLLY: Oh, she can't have everything her own way.

MOMMO: Their inheritance, the three small waiting children, left unattended.

DOLLY (*rooting in her bag, producing a bottle of vodka*): How yeh.

MARY *merely nods, continues working.*

MOMMO: And night fast closing around them.

DOLLY: Stronger she's gettin'. A present.

MARY (*hopeful that the vodka is for her birthday*): For what?

DOLLY: 'Cause I couldn't come up last night.

MARY: What do I! (*want with a bottle of vodka*)

DOLLY: Yeh never know. She'll last forever.

MOMMO: Then, drawing a deep breath. (*She draws a deep breath.*) Oh but didn't give vent to it, for like the man he was I'm sayin', refusing to *sigh,* or submit. An', 'On we go, Pedlar' says he, an' man, horse, cart, and the woman falling in between the two hind shafts set off on the road to Bochtán, which place did not come by its present appellation, Bailegangaire, till that very night. Now.

DOLLY: Jesus, Bailegangaire – D'yeh want a fag? – night after night, can't you stop her. A fag?

MARY (*declines the cigarette*): No.

DOLLY: Night after night the same old story – (*Proffering cigarettes again.*) Ary you might as well.

MARY *ignores her.*

By Jesus I'd stop her.

MARY: I wish you'd stop using that word, Dolly. I've been trying to stop her.

DOLLY: Michaeleen is sick. The tonsils again. So I couldn't come up last night. I'm worried about them tonsils. What d'yeh think? So I can't stay long tonight either.

MARY *sighs.*

MOMMO: But to come to Bailegangaire so ye'll have it all.

MARY: Aren't you going to say hello to her?

DOLLY: What's up with yeh?

MARY: Nothing.

MOMMO: Them from that place had been to the market were 'riving back home.

DOLLY: *Home,* I'm goin'.

MOMMO: One of them, Séamus Costello by name.

MARY: Aren't you going to take off your coat?

DOLLY: What do you mean?

MOMMO: Oh a fine strappin' man.

MARY: What do you mean what do I mean!

DOLLY *turns stubbornly into the fire.*

MOMMO: Wherever he got it from. The size an' the breadth of him, you'd near have to step into the verge to give him sufficient right-of-way. 'Twould be no use him extending the civility 'cause you'd hardly get around him I'm saying. And he was liked. Rabbits he was interested in. This to his widowed mother's dismay, but that's another thing. And the kind of man that when people'd espy him approaching the gurgle'd be already startin' in their mouths – Och-haw. For he was the exception, ye understand, with humour in him as big as himself. And I'm thinkin' he was the one an' only boast they ever had in that cursèd place. What time is it?

MARY } Eight.
DOLLY } Nine.

They look at each other and bygones are bygones.

MARY: Quarter past eight.

MOMMO: Quarter past eight, an' sure that's not late. That's a rhyme. Now for ye! (*She takes a sip of tea.*) Too sweet.

MARY *rectifying the tea situation. A cajoling tone coming into* DOLLY's *voice – there is something on her mind, and she is watching and assessing* MARY *privately.*

DOLLY: They say it's easier to do it for someone else's (*to take care of a stranger*). (*Declining tea which* MARY *offers.*) No thanks. And that old story is only upsetting her, Mary. Isn't it?

MARY *is too intelligent to be taken in by* DOLLY's *tone or tactics – but this is not at issue here: she has other things on her mind. She sits by the fire with* DOLLY *and now accepts the cigarette.* MOMMO *is sipping tea.*

Harping on misery. And only wearing herself out. And you. Amn't I right. Mary? And she never finishes it – Why doesn't she finish it? And have done with it. For God's sake.

MARY *considers this ('Finish it? And have done with it.'), then forgets it for the moment. She is just looking into the fire.*

MARY: I want to have a talk to you, Dolly.

DOLLY (*cautiously*): . . . About what? . . . What?

MARY: Do you remember . . . (*She shakes her head: she does not know.*)

DOLLY: . . . What? . . . I know it affects you. Like, her not reco'nisin' you ever – Why wouldn't it? But you were away a long time.

MARY *looks up: she has been only half listening.*

That's the reason.

MARY: . . . I've often thought . . . (*Just looking at the fire again.*)

DOLLY: . . . What?

MARY: I may have been too – bossy, at first.

DOLLY: Well, well, there could be something in that, too.

MARY: But I wanted to . . . bring about change. Comfort, civilized.

DOLLY: Yes, well, but. Though I don't know. You were away an awful long time. I was left holdin' the can. Like, when yeh think of it, you owe me a very big debt.

MARY (*looks up*): Hmm: A very big?

DOLLY: I mean that's why she reco'nises me.

MARY *looking at the fire again;* DOLLY *watching* MARY. *Something on* DOLLY's *mind; she coughs in preparation to speak –*

MARY: We had a pony and trap once. The Sunday outings. You don't remember?

DOLLY *puzzled shakes her head.*

Ribbons. Grandad would always bring ribbons home for our hair. You don't remember.

DOLLY: . . . You work too hard.

MARY *laughs to herself at the remark.*

DOLLY: (*laughs*): What?

MARY *shakes her head.*

DOLLY: And you're too serious.

MARY: Do you remember Daddy?

DOLLY: Well, the photographs.

They glance at the framed photographs on the wall.

Aul' brown ghosts. (*Playful, but cajoling:*) Y'are, y'are, too serious.

MARY (*eyes back to the fire*): I suppose I am. I don't know what I'm trying to say. (*Sighs.*) Home.

MOMMO (*has put down her cup*): And that, too, is well.

DOLLY: What?

MARY, *another slight shake of her head: she doesn't know.*

MOMMO: And now with his old jiggler of a bicycle set again' the gable, Costello was goin' in to John Mah'ny's, the one and only shop for everything for miles around.

DOLLY (*to* MARY): What?

MOMMO: 'Cold enough for ye, ladies!' Now! Cold enough for ye, ladies. And that was the first remark he was to utter that evening. And the two women he had thus accosted set to gurgling at once and together. 'Caw och-caw, Seamusheen a wockeen, God bless yeh, och-caw' says the old crone that was in it buyin the salt. And, 'Uck-uck-uck, uck-uck hunuka huckina-caw,

Costello' from the young buxom woman tendin' the shop-end of the counter, and she turnin' one of the babes in her arms so that he too could behold the hero. 'Aren't they gettin' awful big, God bless them,' then saying Costello of the two twins an' they gogglin' at him. 'Jack Frost is coming with a vengeance for ye tonight,' says he, 'or the Bogey Man maybe bejingoes'. And to the four or five others now holding tight their mother's apron. 'Well, someone is comin' anyways,' says he, 'if ye all aren't good'. An' then off with him to the end where the drink was.

DOLLY } Good man Josie!
MARY } No!

MOMMO } 'Good man, Josie!'
MARY } Don't encourage her.

MOMMO } Now!
MARY } I'm – ! (*going out of my mind*)

MOMMO } Good man, Josie.
MARY } I'm trying to stop it!

MOMMO } And that was the second greeting he uttered that night.
MARY } Talk to her!
DOLLY } That's what I try to do!

MOMMO: He got no reply.

DOLLY (*going to* MOMMO; *under her breath*): Good man Josie, Jesus!

MOMMO: Nor did he expect one.

DOLLY (*calling back to* MARY): And I'm going at quarter to nine! – Good man, Mommo, how's it cuttin'?

MOMMO: Good man – ! Pardon?

DOLLY: How's the adversary treatin' yeh?

MOMMO (*to herself*): Good man Mommo?

DOLLY: I brought yeh sweets.

MOMMO: There's nothing wrong with me.

DOLLY: I didn't say there was.

MOMMO: An' I never done nothin' wrong.

DOLLY: Sweets!

MARY: Butterscotch, isn't it, Dolly?

MOMMO (*to herself, puzzled again*): Good man – Who?

DOLLY: Butterscotch, I've oceans of money.

MARY: Your favourites.

DOLLY: You like them ones.

MARY: Try one. You (DOLLY) give it to her.

MOMMO: Do I like them ones?

MARY: Suck it slowly.

DOLLY: Gob-stoppers I should have brought her.

MARY: Shh!

DOLLY: You're lookin' fantastic. (*Going back to the fire.*) It'd be a blessing if she went.

MARY (*placatory*): Shh, don't say things like (*that*). Talk to her, come on.

DOLLY: About what? – It's like an oven in here – And I don't understand a word she's sayin'.

MARY: Take off your – (*coat*).

DOLLY: I – don't – want – to – take – off – my! –

MARY: Tell her about the children.

DOLLY: Seafóid, nonsense talk about forty years ago –

MARY: Come on –

DOLLY: And I've enough problems of my own. Why don't you stick her in there? (*One of the other rooms.*)

MARY: It's damp, and she understands – recognises you a lot of the time.

DOLLY *rolling her eyes but following* MARY *back to the bed again.*

Where she can see you.

DOLLY: Well, the children are all fine, Mommo. (*A slip*) Well. Well, Michaeleen is sick, the tonsils again. I've rubber-backed lino in all the bedrooms now, the Honda is going like a bomb and the *lounge*, my dear, is carpeted. I seen the lean and lanky May Glynn, who never comes near ye or this house, in the garden when I was motoring over but she went in without a salute. I must have distemper too, or whatever. Conor, that other lean and lanky bastard, is now snaking his fence in another six inches, and my darlin' old sharp-eyes-and-the-family-rosary, sends her pers'nal blessings to ye both. Now. Darlin's.

MARY: Is she babysitting for you?

DOLLY: No. She is not babysitting for me. I don't want her or any of the McGrath clan in my house. But I have someone babysittin' – since you're lookin' concerned.

MARY: I wasn't.

MOMMO (*sucking the sweet*): They're nice.

DOLLY: An' the cat had kittens. (*To MARY:*) D'yeh want a kitten? Do you, Mommo? (*A touch of sour introversion.*) Does anyone? Before I drown them.

MOMMO: Tom is in Galway.

MARY: Did you hear from Stephen?

DOLLY: The 'wire' again on Friday, regular as clockwork.

MARY: Did you hear, Mommo?

MOMMO: I did. But she told May Glynn not to be waitin', her own mother'd be needin' her, and that they'd be home before dark for sure.

DOLLY: Eighty-five quid a week and never a line.

MARY: He's busy.

DOLLY (*to herself*): Fuck him. I don't know what to do with the money! (*Sudden introspection again.*) Or do I? I've started saving. (*Then impetuously:*) Do *you* want some? Well, do you, Mommo? To go dancin'.

MARY *is laughing at her sister's personality.*

What?

MARY: Stephen will be home as usual for Christmas.

DOLLY: For his goose.

MARY: Won't he, Mommo?

MOMMO (*to herself*): Stephen, yes, fugum.

They laugh. Then, DOLLY *grimly:*

DOLLY: Well maybe it'd be better if the bold Stephen skipped his visit this Christmas. (*Rises and turns her back on them.*) Jesus, misfortunes.

MARY *now wondering, concerned, her eyes on* DOLLY'*s back, the stout figure.*

MOMMO: Yes. Misfortunes.

MARY: . . . Dolly?

DOLLY: Ooh, a cake, a candle – candles! What's the occasion? (*She gives a kiss to* MOMMO.) Well, I'm off now, darlin', an' God an' all his holy saints protect an' bless yeh.

MOMMO (*buried in her own thoughts until now*): When did you arrive?

DOLLY: What?

MOMMO: When did you arrive?

DOLLY: I arrived –

MOMMO: Sure you're welcome, when did you arrive?

DOLLY: I arrived –

MOMMO: Well did yeh?

DOLLY: I did.

MOMMO: From where?

DOLLY: From –

MOMMO: Now. And is that where y'are now?

DOLLY: The very location.

MOMMO: Now! I never knew that. Where?

DOLLY: Ahm . . . Aw Jesus, Mommo, you have us all as confused as yourself! Ballindine, Ball-in-dine.

MOMMO: Hah? Oh yes, yeh told me. Now. Who are you?

DOLLY: Dolly. I think.

MOMMO (*considering this, sucking her sweet*): Now. Dolly.

DOLLY: Dolly!

MOMMO: Yes.

DOLLY: Look, I have to be – (*going*) I'm Dolly, your granddaughter, and that's Mary, your other granddaughter, and your grandson Tom, Tom is dead.

MARY: Shh!

DOLLY: Ar, shh! (*To* MOMMO:) Now do you know?

MOMMO: I do. I'm waiting for someone.

DOLLY: Who're yeh waitin' for?

MOMMO: I'm not tellin' yeh.

DOLLY: A man, is it?

MOMMO (*laughing*) 'Tis.

DOLLY: Och hona ho gus hah-haa, an' what'll he have for yeh?

MOMMO (*laughing*): A big stick.

DOLLY: M-m-m-m-m! – Stick, the bata! Mmmah! (*Sexual innuendo.*) Now! Try that subject on her if you want to stop her.

MOMMO: Oh but they were always after me.

DOLLY: An' did they ketch yeh?

MOMMO: The ones I wanted to.

DOLLY: An' they're still after yeh?

MOMMO: But I bolt the door – on some of them. (*Laughing.*)

DOLLY (*to* MARY): That's what all the aul ones like to talk about. I think you're goin' soft in the head.

MOMMO (*recognising her*): Is it Dolly? Aw is it my Dolly! Well, d'yeh know I didn't rec'nise yeh. Sure you were always the joker. Aw, my Dolly, Dolly, Dolly, come 'ere to me.

DOLLY *hesitates, is reluctant, then succumbs to the embrace; indeed, after a moment she is clinging tightly to the old woman.*

MARY *stands by, isolated, but watching the scene. She would love to be included. The smallest gesture of affection or recognition would help greatly.*

Ah. lovee. Lovee, lovee, lovee. Sure if I knew you were comin' – (*Aside to* MARY:) Will you put on the kettle, will you? Standing there! – I'd've baked a cake. That's an old one. Oh, mo pheata (*my pet*). Why didn't you send word? An' you got fat. You did! On me oath! Will you put on the kettle, Miss, will you! (*Whispering.*) Who is that woman?

DOLLY (*tearfully, but trying to joke*): She's the sly one.

MOMMO: She is. (*Loudly, hypocritically:*) Isn't she nice?

DOLLY: Watch her.

MARY *goes off to another room.*

MOMMO: Why is she interfering?

DOLLY: Shh, Mommo.

MOMMO: Be careful of that one.

DOLLY: I'm in terrible trouble.

MOMMO: Yes, watch her.

DOLLY (*extricating herself from the embrace, brushing away a tear*): Leave her to me. I'll deal with her. (*Calls:*) Miss! Will you come out, will you, an' make a brew! An' put something in it! Sure you should know about all kinds of potions.

MARY *has returned with a suitcase. She places it somewhere.*

. . . Someone going on a *voyage?*

MARY: I have to come to a decision, Dolly.

DOLLY: Again?

MARY: She's your responsibility too.

DOLLY: I know you think I inveigled you back here so that Stephen and I could escape.

MARY: No one inveigled me anywhere. You're not pulling your weight.

DOLLY (*shrugs*): There's always the County Home.

MARY: You –

DOLLY: Wouldn't I? Why should I stick myself again back in here?

MARY: Why should I?

DOLLY: In a place like this.

MARY: Why do I? In a place like this.

DOLLY (*shrugs*): That's your business. Well, I have to be going.

MARY: I'd like to go out sometimes too.

DOLLY: For a 'walk'? *Home*, I'm going.

MARY: You look it.

DOLLY: Alright: I'll tell you, so that you can go, where the man is waiting.

MARY: Man? Men!

DOLLY *shrugs, is moving off.*

I need to talk to – someone!

DOLLY (*her back to* MARY; *quietly*): I need to talk to someone too.

MARY (*an insinuation*): Why don't you take off your coat?

DOLLY (*faces* MARY; *a single solemn nod of her head; then*): Because, now, I am about to leave. I'll figure out something. I might even call back, 'cause it doesn't take long, does it? Just a few minutes; that's all it takes.

MARY: You're disgusting.

DOLLY: Am I?

MARY (*going to one of the other rooms*): I've *come* to a decision. (*Off.*) County Home! You won't blackmail me!

DOLLY (*to herself*): I hate this house. (*To* MOMMO:) Good man Josie! (*Going out; an undertone:*) Ah, fuck it all.

MOMMO: Oh yes. 'Good man, Josie!' Now! Good man Josie. And that was the second greeting Costello was to utter that evening.

MARY (*coming in*): I'll leave everything here for you spic and span, of course.

She has not heard DOLLY *go out; now she stands there looking at the door, the motorcycle outside driving away, arms outstretched, her hands clapping together some of her wardrobe (as if demonstrating the possibility that she is leaving rather than confirming it).*

MOMMO: He got no reply. Nor did he expect one. For Josie was a Greaney and none was ever right in that fambly.

MARY (*to herself*): It's not fair.

MOMMO: An' the threadbare fashion'ry, not a top-coat to him, the shirt neck open.

MARY (*to herself*): Not a gansey.

MOMMO: Nor a gansey.

MARY: *Nor* a gansey. (*Calling after* DOLLY:) Stephen called me 'dearest'!

MOMMO: An' the tuthree raggedy top-coats on the others.

MARY: Wanted to have a child by me!

MOMMO: An' some with extra sacking bandaging around them.

MARY: A girl, he said, so that she'd look like me.

MOMMO: Though some say he had the knack of mendin' clocks, if he had.

MARY: But you'll never know a thing about it!

MOMMO: And none ever bested him at Ride-the-Blind-Donkey. (*She has a sip of tea.*) What's in this? Miss?

MARY: Your husband wined and dined and bedded me! (*Realising she has been talking to the door.*) I'm going soft in the head.

MOMMO: Miss!

MARY: The County Home! (*Gesturing, meaning did* MOMMO *hear what* DOLLY *said.*)

MOMMO: Hot drink, decent supa tea!

MARY (*automatically sets about making fresh tea, then she stops*): I have *come* to a decision I said. Do you understand? So if you could wait a moment. (*She starts to discard some of the clothes, packing others; talking to herself again.*) Just to see who is in earnest this time. I sit there.

MOMMO ⎫ Me mouth is dry d'ye know.

MARY ⎭ I just sit there. And I was doing well – I was the success! Now I'm talking to myself. And I *will* leave the place spic and span.

MOMMO: Howandever. 'How the boys!' was Costello's third greeting. This time to two old men with their heads in the chimbley, each minding a pint of black porter, before Costello's coming in, were in no heed or hurry to be drinkin'. The one of them givin' out the odd sigh, smoking his pipe with assiduity and beating the slow obsequies of a death-roll with his boot. An' the other, a Brian by name, replying in sagacity 'Oh yis,' sharing the silent mysteries of the world between them. Me mouth is (*dry*), d'ye know.

MARY: Just a moment! (*Going to another room.*) Dependent on a pension and that bitch.

MOMMO: Where is she? Miss!

MARY (*off*): Miss! Miss is coming. (*Entering with more clothes.*) Miss: as if I didn't exist. That's the thanks I get – (*Winces to herself.*) It's – not – thanks I'm looking for. (*Absently*:) What am I looking for, Mommo? I had to come home. No one inveigled me. I wanted to come home.

MOMMO: Put it down, put it down!

MARY: Why can't you be civil to me? At least tonight.

MOMMO: Put it down! (*She continues her story.*)

MARY, *exasperated, comes out of her reverie, dumps the clothes and sets about making more tea.*

MARY: And you know very well who I am! You do! You do!

MOMMO: Sure it's often I'd be watchin' me own father engaged in the same practice, drawing wisdom from the fire. 'Deed, on one such occasion, an' twas maybe after a full hour's contemplation, he craned his neck, the glaze to his eyes, to accost me with the philosophy that was troublin' him. 'How much does a seagull weigh?' I held my silence to be sure, for times he'd get cross – oh he'd welt yeh with the stick – if a guess was attempted or a sound itself uttered. For he wouldn't be talkin' to you at all. The groans out of that man decipherin' the enigma. Then, at last, when he found for himself the answer to the riddle he declared in 'sured solemnity, 'I'm thinking' who I'm waitin' for. Oh, men have their ways an' women their places an' that is God's plan, my bright ones.

She gets out of bed. MARY sees her and is hurrying to her assistance.

Shthap!

MARY *is stopped by the ferocity. MOMMO squats, hidden behind the headboard of the bed.*

MARY: . . . And to change your nightdress . . . I was a nurse, Mommo . . . And other offers of marriage . . . Plenty of them!

Then, quickly, she takes the opportunity of re-making the bed.

Wined and dined and bedded me. But I told him to keep away from me, to stop following me, to keep away from here.

She replaces the sheets with clean ones, removes the bed-warmer – which is a cast-iron lid of a pot in a knitted woollen cover: she puts the lid into the fire to reheat it. She appears almost happy when she is working constructively. She recites as she works.

'There is the silence of copse or croft
When the wind sinks dumb.
And of belfry loft
When the tenor after tolling stops its hum.'

And sure you have lots of poems. lots of stories, nice stories, instead of that old one. 'Mick Delaney' – do you remember that one? We loved that one. How did it begin? Or ghost stories. People used to come *miles* to hear you tell stories. Oh! and do you remember: the gramophone. Yes, we had a gramophone too. 'The banshee is out tonight go down (*on*) your knees and say your prayers – Wooooo!' Or would you like me to read you a story?

MOMMO (*reappearing from behind the bed*): Heh heh heh heh!

MARY (*now her solemn grave face*): There was happiness here too, Mommo. Harmony?

MOMMO (*straight back, neck craned*): You can be going now, Miss.

MARY: . . . Alright.

She takes the chamberpot from behind the headboard of the bed and goes out. We can see her outside, motionless; a little later, continuing motionless except for the movements of smoking a cigarette.

MOMMO: She knows too much about our business entirely. (*She calls hypocritically.*) And thank you! (*Giggles getting back into the bed.*) Now amn't I able for them? (*Sings.*) 'Once I loved with fond affection, all my thoughts they were in thee, till a dork (*dark*) haired girl deceived me – ' Ye like that one. But now that

Costello was in it the aspect was
transforming. 'An',' says old Brian,
taking his head out of the fire, 'What's
the news from the Big World?' 'The
Dutch has taken Holland!' says
Costello with such a rumble out of him
near had the whole house shook
asunder and all in it in ululation so
infectious was the sound. Save Josie
who was heedless, but rapping with
severity on the counter for more
libation. And 'John!' says the young
buxom woman, calling to her husband
– 'John' – to come out and tend his
end of the counter, an' she now putting
questions on bold Costello.
   'You wor in Tuam?' says she, 'I was
'You wor in Tuam?' says she, 'I was
in Tuam,' says he. 'Yeh wor?' says she,
'I was,' says he. 'An' how was it?' says
she.
   'Well, not tellin' you a word of a lie
now,' says he 'but 'twas deadly'.
   And 'Ory!' says the crone that was in
it buyin' the salt.
   'Did yeh hear?' says the young
buxom woman to her husband. John,
to be sure. He had 'rived from the
kitchen an' was frownin' pullin' pints.
Merchants d'ye know: good market or
bad, the arithmetic in the ledger has to
come out correct. An' the multifarious
diversifications in matters of local
commerce, the head had to be working
perpetually.
   'Well do yeh tell me so?' says the
young buxom woman.
   'I do tell yeh so,' says Costello.
'Talkin' about a Maragadh Mór? – I
never in all me born days seen light or
likes of it!'
   Now they were listening.

MARY *comes in, washes and replaces
the chamberpot. She selects her 'going-
away' suit from the second bundle of
clothes which she brought from the
other room and, trying the waist against
herself, she puts the suit on a chair
beside the fire to air it. She leaves her
clothes to go out twice through the
following and bring in two armsful of
turf.*

MOMMO: 'Firkins of butter,' says he,
'an' cheese be the hundred-weight.
Ducks, geese, chickens, bonavs and –
Geese!' says he, 'geese! There was
hundreds of them! There was hundreds

of them! There was hundreds upon
hundreds of thousands of them! The
ground I tell ye was white with them!'
   And 'White with them,' says the
crone.
   'They went ch-cheap then?' says
John, still bowed frownin' over the
tricks of pullin' porter.
   'Cheap then?' says Costello, 'sure
yeh couldn't give them away sure. Sure
the sight of so many chickens an' geese
an'! Sure all the people could do was
stand an' stare.'
   'They were puzzled,' says the crone.
   'I'm tellin' yeh,' says Costello,
'Napoleon Bonaparte wouldn't have
said no to all the provisions goin' a-
beggin' in that town of Tuam today.'
   An' 'Hah?' says John, squintin', the
head-work interrupted.
   'On his retreat from Moscow, sure,'
says Costello.
   'Or Josephine – Wuw! – neither.'
Now! Wuw. Them were his ways, an'
he off rumblin' again: 'Oh, I'm a bold
bachelor aisy an' free, both city and
country is aiqual to me!' having the
others equivalently pursuant: 'Wo ho
ho, wo ho ho!'
   'But you sis-sold the rabbits, d-did
yeh, Costello?' says John. An' wasn't
there a gap. Oh, only for the second.
'Oh I sold them,' then sayin' Costello.
'Oh I did, did,' saying he. 'Oh on me
solemn 'n dyin' oath! Every man-jack-
rabbit of them.' Like a man not to be
believed, his bona fides in question.
   'Yeh-yeh c-odjer yeh-yeh,' says
John. Whatever he meant. But he wa⌐
not at all yet feeling cordial.
   But thus was the night faring into its
progression, others 'riving back home
an' how did they do an' who else was
in it, did they buy e'er a thing, Costello
settin' them laughin', John frownin' an'
squintin', an' the thief of a Christmas
they wor all goin' t'have. What're ye
doin' there?

MARY *is stacking the turf near the fire.
She holds up a sod of turf to show*
MOMMO.

Hah? . . . There's nothing here for
people to be prying in corners for.

MARY *holds up the woollen cover of
the bed-warmer.*

Hah? . . . Bring in the brishen of turf

an' then you may be goin' home to your own house.

MARY: . . . Alright.

She moves as if going out back door, then moves silently to the comparative dark of the far corner of the room where she remains motionless.

MOMMO: You couldn't be up to them.

MARY *continues silent. She is trying a new ploy, hoping* MOMMO *will stop, will sleep.*

Isn't life a strange thing too? 'Tis. An' if we could live it again? . . . Would we? (*live it differently*) In harmony? Aah, I don't know. (*She yawns.*) Oh ho huneo! An' 'twas round about now the rattlin' of the horse an' cart was heard evidential abroad an' had them peepin' at the windy. 'Twas the decent man an' his decent wife the same was in it. And 'Stand, Pedlar,' says the man in (*a*) class of awesome whisper. And his decent wife from the heel of the cart to his side to view the spectre was now before them. The aspect silver of moon an' stars reflecting off the new impossibility. Loughran's Hill. Creature. She now clutching more tightly the sweets to her breast. Switch off that aul' thing (*the radio*), there's nothing on it. (*She yawns again: her eyes close.*)

They were silent a while.

MARY (*whispers*): Sleep.

MOMMO (*eyes open*): Hah? (*Looking around.*) *Now* what was there for doing? Which way to cast the hopeful eye. No-no, not yet, in deliberate caution, would he acknowledge the shop, John Mah'ny's, forninst them. But looked behind him the road they came, forward again, but to what avail? There was only John Mah'ny's now for his deep contemplation, nature all around them serenely waiting, and didn't the two little smiles come appearing again.

MOMMO *slides a little down the bed.*

MARY (*whispers*): Sleep.

MOMMO: Hah?

MARY: Sleep, sleep. Peace, peace.

MOMMO (*yawns*): An' the strangers,

that decent man an' his decent wife the same, were rounding the gable into the merchant's yard, an' sorry the night that was the decision. What time is it? . . . She's gone. An' she can stay gone. But them are the details, c'rrect to the particular. And they can be vouched for. For there was to be many's the inquisition by c'roner, civic guard and civilian on all that transpired in John Mah'ny's that night. Now. Wasn't that a nice story? An' we'll all be goin' to sleep.

She is asleep.

Tommy O'Brien's programme is over (or nearly over): it is followed by an announcement of what The Sunday Concert *is going to be later on: 'A Shubert Evening, Symphony No. 9, 'The Great', followed by 'Notturno' in E Flat. But now we have* Archives *presented by . . .' etc.*

MARY *continues motionless for some moments.*

A car passes by outside.

MARY (*looking at* MOMMO): Sleep? For how long? . . .

She switches off the radio. She switches off the lights. She goes to the table and idly starts lighting three or four of the candles on the cake, using a new match to light each successive candle.

(*To herself:*) Give me my freedom, Mommo . . . What freedom? . . . No freedom without structure . . . Where can I go? . . . How can I go (*Looking up and around at the rafters.*) with all this? (*She has tired of her idle game of lighting the candles.*) . . . And it didn't work before for me, did it? . . . I came back.

(*To herself, and idly at first:*) Now as all do know . . . Now as all do know . . . Now as all do know the world over the custom when entering the house of another – be the house public, private with credentials or no – is to invoke our Maker's benediction on all present. (*Adds a piece of sardonic humour:*) Save the cat. Well, as the Bailegangaires would have it later, no mention of our Maker, or His Blessed Son, was mentioned as the strangers came 'cross that threshel (*threshold*). But no, no, no, no, no. No now! They

were wrongin' that couple. (*To the
sleeping* MOMMO:) Weren't they?
They wor. They were. (*To* MOMMO:)
And when you. And when that decent
woman gave the whole story to her
father, what did he say? (*A touch of
mimicry of* MOMMO:) An' believe
you me he knew all about them. That
the Bailegangaires were a venomous
pack of jolter-headed gobshites. Didn't
he? He did. Now for yeh! An ill-bred
band of amadáns an' oinseachs,
untutored in science, philosophy or the
fundamental rudimentaries of
elementary husbandry itself. A low
crew of illiterate plebs, drunkards and
incestuous bastards, and would ever
continue as such – (*Holds up her finger
to correct her wording.*) and would ever
continue as *much*, improper and
despicable in their incorrigibility. Them
were his words. Weren't they? They
wor. They're not nice, he said. Supa
tea. (*Short sardonic laugh as she pours
a glass of vodka for herself.*) And he
was the man to give the tongue-lashin'.
An' 'twas from him I got my learnin'.
Wasn't it? That's who I'm waitin' for.
(*She has a sip of the vodka.*) Too
sweet. (*She dilutes the vodka with
water.*) Me father. He has a big stick.
That's where security lies. (*She has a
drink: then, whimpering as* MOMMO
might.) I wanta go home, I wanta go
home. (*New tone, her own, frustrated:*)
So do I, so do I. *Home.* (*Anger.*)
Where is it, Mommo?

*Then she is sorry for her anger. She
pulls herself together for a few
moments. The silence now being
punctuated by a car passing by outside.*

A lot of activity tonight. And all
weekend.

MARY *picks up her book but does not
open it.*

'There is the silence of copse or croft

*She starts to pace the periphery of the
room.*

'When the wind sinks dumb.
And of belfry loft
When the tenor after tolling stops its
    hum.

'And there's the silence of a lonely
    pond
Where a man was drowned . . .'

*She stops for a moment or two looking
at one of the framed photographs.*

Where a man, and his brother who
went to save him . . . were drowned.
Bury them in pairs, it's cheaper.

Continues pacing.

'Nor nigh nor yond
No newt, toad, frog to make the
smallest sound.

'But the silence of an empty house
Where oneself was born,
Dwelt, held carouse . . .'

    Did we? Hold carouse.

'With friends
Is of all silence most forlorn.

'It seems no power can waken it – '

Another car passes by. MARY's
reaction to the car:

Come in! 'Or rouse its rooms,
Or the past permit
The present to stir a torpor like a
tomb's.'
Bla bla bla bla bla, like a tomb's. (*To
the book, and dumping it.*) Is that so?
Well, I don't agree with you . . . What
time is it? Twenty past nine . . . Going
crazy. (*Then, on reflection:*) No I'm
not. (*Then suddenly to* MOMMO:)
Wake up *now*, Mommo. Mommo!
Because I don't want to wait till
midnight, or one or two or three
o'clock in the morning, for more of
your – unfinished symphony. I'm ready
now. (*She switches on the light.*) .
Mommo, the cursèd paraffin! (*She
switches on the radio.*) What else did
your father say when you gave him the
story? That many's the one's son or
daughter married into that place went
mental after and had to be took away,
sullyin' and bringin' disgrace on a line
that had been clean up to then, maybe
both sides! What else did he say?
(MOMMO *is awake.*) What about the
snails? What about the earwigs?

MOMMO: 'Oh never step on a snail,' he
intoned.

MARY: 'Nor upon the silver trail he
leaves behind.'

MOMMO: 'For your boot is unworthy.'

MARY: Now!

MOMMO: 'For the snail knows his

place,' he groaned, 'and understands the constant parameters – and the need for parameters – in the case under consideration, God's prize piece, the earth. And therefore the snail is free, and all he does is in innocence.' He did.

MARY: On with the story.

MOMMO: 'D'yeh consider,' says he – the fierce eyes of that man rolling – 'that God designed all this for the likes of the gobshite Bochtáns and their antics?'

MARY: Or for the likes of ourselves?

MOMMO: Or for the likes of ourselves. He did. Them wor his words. That's who I'm waitin' for.

MARY: To continue. But that decent man and his decent wife the same did as was proper on entering.

MOMMO: Sure we weren't meant to be here at all!

MARY: The customary salutation was given.

MOMMO: That was one of God's errors.

MARY: Though silently, for they were shy people, and confused in their quandry. Mommo? And then, without fuss, the man indicated a seat in the most private corner.

MOMMO: An' they were wrongin' them there again! So they wor.

MARY: They were.

MOMMO: They wor. The whispers bein' exchanged were *not* of malevolent disposition. Yis! – to be sure! – that woman! – Maybe! – had a distracted look to her. Hadn't she reason?

MARY: The Bailegangaires gawpin' at them.

MOMMO: They knew no better.

MARY: Where would they learn it.

MOMMO: Oh-ho, but he bet them – Och hona ho gus hah-haa! – he bet the best of them! . . . Incestuous bastards. (*Absently asking:*) Cigarette. 'An' I caught Tom playin' with the mangler the other evenin', his feet dancin' in the cup.' That's what she was whisperin'. And he lookin' round. 'Not at all, not at all,' tryin' to look pleasant

in the house of another. 'An' won't they have to light the lamp?' That's what she was whisperin'. 'Not at all, not at all,' still lookin' for the place to put his eyes. 'Isn't Mary a big girl now an' well able to look after them.' That's what he was whisperin'. 'An' won't May Glynn be lookin' in on them.' That's what he was whisperin'. But she'd told May Glynn that mornin' not to be waitin', her mother'd be needin' her to look after her young brothers, an' they'd be home before dark for sure. And-sure-she-was-gettin'-on-his-nerves! Till he had to go an' leave her there to a quiet spot at the counter . . . Sure she should've known better. An' she's sorry now. She is. She is. (*Whimpering.*) I wanta see mah father.

MARY *coming to comfort her.*

Shthap! . . . (*Whimpering.*) I wanta go home. (*Warning* MARY; *at the same time taking the cigarette which* MARY *is offering her.*) And he has a big stick.

MARY: I'm not trying to stop you, Mommo.

MOMMO: An' he won't try to stop me. Heh heh heh heh. (*She puffs at the cigarette and then winks wisely at the imagined children at the foot of the bed.*) Men long-married to tearful women are no use to them, my bright ones. But are apt to get cross, and make matters worse, when they can't see the solution. (*She becomes aware of the cigarette.*) What's this? An' who asked for this?

MARY (*taking cigarette from her*): I'm not stopping you. And I just had an idea.

MOMMO } Me mouth is burned.
MARY   } We'll do it together.

Speaking simultaneously:

MOMMO: Rubbishy cigarettes – spendin' money on rubbishy cigarettes–

MARY: We'll finish it. What is it but an old auld story? I'm not stopping you –

MOMMO (*singing: her defiance to* MARY): 'Once I loved with fond affection – '

MARY: And if we finished it, that would be something at least, wouldn't it?

MOMMO: 'All my thoughts they were in thee.'

MARY: Wouldn't it?

MOMMO: 'And no more he thought of me.' (*She lapses into silence. she grows drowsy, or feigns drowsiness.*)

MARY (*singing*): 'Tooralloo ralloo ralladdy, tooralloo ralloo rallee, till a dark – (*Corrects herself:*) dork haired girl deceived me, and no more thought of me' . . . I'll help you, Mommo.

MOMMO: Tom is in Galway. He's afeared of the gander.

MARY: Don't go to sleep. And don't be pretending to sleep either. And what'll you be havin', says John Mahony the proprietor. But the stranger was now puzzlin' something in his brain, he taking in the laughter and Costello's great bellow dominating over all.

   'A lotta noise an' little wool as the devil says shearin' the pig!' sayin' Costello. Wo ho ho! 'An what'll you be havin', Mister,' says John Mahony again. 'A little drop of whiskey an' a small port wine.' And readying the drinks up above says John, 'the frost is determined to make a night of it?' Says he.

   'Behell I don't know,' says old Brian, like the nestor long ago, 'comin' on duskess there was a fine roll of cloud over in the west and if you got the bit of a breeze at all I'm thinkin' you'd soon see a thaw.' And the stranger had produced his purse and was suspended-paused takin' in the forecast. But the two little smiles appearing again, the compendium of his deliberations was that such good fortune as a thaw was not to be. Then – and with a deft enough flick – he pitched the coin on the counter, like a man rejecting all fortune. Good enough.

   He took the drink to his decent wife and was for sitting next to her again but wasn't her head now in and out of the corner and she startin' the cryin'.

MOMMO: She should have known better.

MARY: So what could he do but leave her there again.

MOMMO: An' the church owed him money.

MARY: Did it?

MOMMO (*growls*): The-church-owed-him-money. Oh, the church is slow to pay out. But if you're givin', there's nothin' like money to make them fervent! There's nothin' like money t'make the clergy devout.

MARY: Yes?

MOMMO (*drowsily*): And I'm thinkin', that decent man of late was given to reviewin' the transpirations since his birth . . . But if he was itself, wasn't his decent wife the same? . . . At the end of her tether . . . They were acquainted with grief . . . They wor . . . They wor. Switch off that aul' thing (*the radio*) . . . They wor.

MARY: . . . Mommo? (*She has turned the volume down a bit.*) I know you're pretending. Mommo?

The silence again.

They were acquainted with grief . . . Alright, I won't just help you, I'll do it for you. (*Progressively she begins to dramatise the story more:*) Now John Mahony. (*She corrects her pronunciation:*) Now John Mah'ny was noticing the goings-on between the two and being the proprietor he was possessed of the licence for interrogating newses. And 'you have a distance to go, Mister?' says he. (*Corrects herself again:*) 'You have a d-distance teh-teh g-go, *Mister*?' says he at the stranger. An' says Grandad. An' says the stranger, class of frownin', 'Would that big man down there,' says he, 'be a man by the name of Costello?' And, 'Th-that's who he is,' says John. 'D'yeh know him?' 'No,' says the stranger, in curious introspection. An' 'No' says he again – *still* puzzled in the head. 'But that's a fine laugh.' 'Oh 'tis a f-fine laugh right enough,' says John, 'Hah?' Knowin' more was comin' but hadn't yet reached the senses. And the stranger now drawin' curlicues with his glass upon the counter! Then says he, 'I heard that laugh a wintry day two years ago across the market square in Ballindine, an' I had t'ask a man who he was.' 'Yeh had,' says John. 'I had,' says the stranger, still drawin' the curlicues, an' now admiring his own artistry. An' John was in suspense. And then, of a suddenness, didn't the frown go disappearin' up the stranger's cap. He had it at last. 'Well,' says he – Oh, lookin' the merchant between the two eyes. 'Well,' says he, 'I'm a better laugher than your Costello.'

What time is it? Half-nine. *Someone will come yet. 'Nother supa milk (Short laugh to herself as she gets another glass of vodka.)* Well, I'm a better laugher than your Costello. *(She swallows the drink.)* Now the merchant betrayed nothing. He was well-versed in meeting company, an' all he did was nod the once – *(She nods.)* and then, quick enough of him, referred the matter. And 'Sh-Sheamus!' says he, 'Sh-Sh-Sheamus!' callin' Costello to come down.

She is now listening to the 'putt-putt' of the motorcycle approaching.

A mortal laughing competition there would be.

MARY *now into action, putting away her glass, switching off the radio, getting needle, thread, scissors and the skirt of her 'going-away' suit to take in the waist.*

I knew some one would call. Dolly. Again! I wonder why. *(Cynically.)* Bringing tidings of great joy.

MARY *is seated by the fire.*

DOLLY *comes in. She stretches herself. (She has had her sex in ditch, doorway, old shed or wherever.) She takes in the packed suitcase but as usual leaves such baiting topics until it suits her.*

DOLLY: I have it all figured out.

MARY: The County Home?

DOLLY: Well, maybe nothing as drastic as that. That's a nice suit.

MARY *(does not lift her head from her work)*: Kill her?

DOLLY *(a sideways twist of the head – 'Kill her?' – a more feasible suggestion)*: Can I have a drop of this? *(vodka.)*

MARY: You brought it.

DOLLY *(produces two bottles of mixers)*: I forgot the mixers earlier. In my haste. *(She pours two drinks.)* We might as well have a wake, an

American wake for yeh.

MARY: Not for me. I had a little one, thank you.

DOLLY: You had *two* little ones. (*Puts drink beside* MARY:) Vodka and white. It's a long time since I seen you wearing that.

MARY: Saw.

DOLLY: What?

MARY: I wore it coming home

DOLLY: Did you have to let out the waist?

MARY: I have to take *in* my things. *(A gesture of invitation.)* You need to talk to someone.

DOLLY: Go on: cheers! Since you're off. Are yeh?

MARY *(does not drink, does not look up but lifts her glass and puts it down again)*: Cheers!

DOLLY: And it often crossed my mind the years Stephen and I were here with herself. Kill her. And it wouldn't be none of your fancy nurses' potions either. Get them out of bed, the auld reliable, start them walkin'. Walk the heart out of them. No clues left for coroner or Dr Paddy. And that's how many's the one met their Waterloo. What's the matter?

MARY *shakes her head; just when she does not want to, she is about to break into tears.*

. . . What? . . . Joking . . . I have it all figured out.

MARY *is crying.*

What's the matter?

MARY: Stop it, Dolly.

DOLLY: Mary?

MARY: Leave me alone. *(To get away from* DOLLY *she goes to the radio and switches it on.)* Leave me alone.

DOLLY: What's the . . . Why are you . . . *(She emits a few whimpers.)* Mary?

MOMMO *(has woken up and is watching them suspiciously)*: Heh heh heh heh.

DOLLY: Good man Josie! *(And immediately back to* MARY:) Mary? Why are you? Don't.

MOMMO: What's the plottin' an' whisperin' for?

DOLLY: Good man Josie! (*And immediately back to* MARY *again*:) What? (*Crying.*) What? . . . Don't. Please. (*Her arms around* MARY.)

They are all speaking at once. MARY *and* DOLLY *crying.*

MOMMO: Oh yes. 'Good man, Josie. Now! Good man Josie. And that was the second greeting he uttered that night.

DOLLY: What? . . . Shh! . . . What?

MARY: I don't know. I don't know.

MOMMO: He got no reply. Nor did he expect one. For Josie was a Greaney an' none was ever right in that fambly.

MARY: I wanted to come home.

DOLLY: What?

MARY: I had to come home.

MOMMO: An' the threadbare fashion'ry, not a top-coat to him, the shirt neck open, nor a gansey.

DOLLY: What?

MARY: This is our home.

DOLLY: I know.

MARY: This is our home.

DOLLY: I know.

MARY (*pulling away from* DOLLY *to shout at* MOMMO:) Finish it, finish it, that much at least –

MOMMO: Och hona ho gus hah-haa! –

MARY: Have done with it! – that much at least!

MOMMO: Och hona ho gus hah-haa!

MARY (*to* DOLLY *who is following her*): Why don't you take off your coat! (*To* MOMMO:) What was waiting for them at dawn when they got home in the morning?

MARY*'s remark to* DOLLY *has stopped* DOLLY *for a moment, but* DOLLY *comes to* MARY *and puts her arms around her again, the two of them crying through to the end.*
  And MOMMO *has not given way to the above, continuing without pause.*

MOMMO: Wo ho ho! – Heh heh heh! Wo ho ho! – Heh heh heh! – an' the tuthree raggedy top-coats on the others! – The poor an' neglected, the wretched an' forlorn – 'Twas the best night ever! – the impoverished an' hungry, eyes big as saucers, howlin' their defiance at the heavens through the ceilin' – Och hona ho gus hah-haa! – inviting of what else might come or care to come! Wo ho ho – Heh heh heh . . . (*Quietening down.*) Though some say he had the knack of mendin' clocks, if he had. And none ever bested him at Ride-the-Blind-Donkey. Howandever. 'How the boys!' was Costello's third greeting, this time to two old men with their heads in the chimbley . . .

The lights fading through the above and music up – 'Notturno'.

ACT TWO

*'Notturno' introducing Act Two: this
being superimposed by the announcement
for* The Sunday Concert *on the radio
together with* MOMMO's *voice continuing
her story.* MOMMO *has arrived at and is
repeating the last section of the story
where* MARY *left off in Act One.
A sniff from* MARY, *her tears are all
but finished. Both she and* DOLLY *have
their 'vodkas and white' and a slice of the
birthday cake on plates beside them.*
MARY *is examining a small computerised
gadget.*

MOMMO: . . . 'yeh had', says John. 'I
   had' says the stranger, still drawin' the
   curlicues an' admiring his own artistry.

MARY: What is it? (*the gadget*)

DOLLY: I don't know. Happy birthday!

MOMMO: An' John was in suspense.
   An' then of a suddenness didn't the
   frown go disappearing up the stranger's
   cap. He had it at last.

MARY: It's not a calculator.

DOLLY: Data processing thing from the
   plant above.

MARY: You didn't get a handbook?

DOLLY: I got it off one of the lads
   working in the – You're the brainy
   one.

MOMMO: 'Well,' says he – oh lookin'
   the merchant between the two eyes –
   'Well,' says he, 'I'm a better laugher
   than your Costello.'

DOLLY: Give it to her if you like.

MARY: No (*it is precious: a present*) I'm
   sorry for. (*Crying.*)

A car passes by outside.

DOLLY: Ar – Phhh – don't be silly. Did
   yeh see the helicopter on Friday? The
   plant, they say, is for closure. The
   Chinese are over.

MARY: Japanese. (*Her attention now
   returning to* MOMMO.)

MOMMO: Now the merchant betrayed
   nothing.

DOLLY: I prefer to call them Chinese.
   (*Watching* MARY *go to* MOMMO.)

DOLLY's *mind beginning to tick over
on how to present her 'proposition' to*
MARY. MARY's *nervous energy, after
the lull, setting her to work again:
washing her plate, removing the bed-
warmer from the fire and slipping it into
the bed at* MOMMO's *feet, wrapping
up the cake in tinfoil and putting it
away, stoking the fire . . . but,
predominantly, her eyes, concentration,
always returning to* MOMMO; *a
resoluteness increasing to have
Mommo's story finished.*

MOMMO: He was well-versed at
   meeting company. And all he did was
   nod the once. (*She nods solemnly.*)

DOLLY: I must get a set of decent glasses
   for you the next time I'm in town.

MOMMO: Then, quick enough of him,
   referred the matter.

DOLLY: And I'm sure there's rats in
   that thatch.

MOMMO: An' 'Sh-Sheamus!' says he.

DOLLY: I could see Hallilan the
   contractor about slatin' it.

MOMMO: 'Sh-Sheamus!' Calling
   Costello to come down.

DOLLY: What d'yeh think?

MARY: Shhh!

MOMMO: A laughing competition there
   would be.

DOLLY (*puzzled by* MARY's
   behaviour): And I was thinking of
   getting her a doll.

MARY (*eyes fastened on* MOMMO): No,
   let's see if she'll continue.

DOLLY: What?

MARY: Good enough. Then down steps
   the bold Costello.

MOMMO: Pardon? (*And instead of
   continuing, she starts singing:*) 'Once I
   loved with fond affection, all my
   thoughts they were in thee, till a dork
   haired gurl deceived me, and no more
   he thought of me.'

MARY (*through Mommo's song,
   returning to the fire, all the time looking
   at* MOMMO): Down steps the bold
   Costello. You have some suggestion,
   something figured out.

DOLLY: What?

MARY: She's going to finish it.

DOLLY: Finish it? Why?

MARY: I don't know, I can't do anything the way things are.

MOMMO: Now. Ye like that one.

DOLLY: I thought you were trying to stop her. Sit down.

MARY: She's going to finish it –

DOLLY: You're always on your feet –

MARY: *Tonight!*

DOLLY: I want to have a chat. Another drink?

MARY (*mechanically about to pour drinks, stops*): No. A laughing competition there *will* be! (*And goes to* MOMMO:) Then down steps the bold Costello.

MOMMO: Pardon?

MARY: Then down steps the bold Costello.

MOMMO: Oh yes.

DOLLY: Well, as a matter of fact, I do have a proposition.

MARY: Shhh!

MOMMO: Then down steps the bold Costello. And 'Hah?' says he, seeing the gravity on the proprietor's mien. But the proprietor – John, to be sure – referred him like that (*She nods in one direction.*). An 'Hah?' says Costello, lookin' at the stranger. But weren't the two eyes of the stranger still mildly fixed on John, an' 'Hah?' says Costello lookin' back at John. But, there was no countin' John's cuteness. He takes the two steps backwards, then the one step to the sidewards slidin' his arse along the shelf to 'scape the strangers line of vision an' demonstrate for all his neutrality in the matter. 'Hah!' poor Costello goin', 'Hah!' to the one. 'Hah!' to the other – 'Hah!' 'Hah!' – the head swung near off his neck, an' now wonderin' I'm sure what on earth he'd done wrong – 'Hah!' – an' 'twas a bailey in disguise maybe was the small little stranger. Costello was a delightful poacher.

DOLLY: Mary? (*Topping up the drinks.*)

MOMMO: An' no help from John. Puffing a tuneless whistle at the ceiling!

DOLLY: I have a proposition.

MOMMO: 'Phuh-phuh-phuh-phuh.' (*John's tuneless whistle.*)

MARY (*absently accepting drink*): Phuh-phuh-phuh-phuh.

MOMMO: Then says the stranger –

DOLLY (*to herself*): Jesus!

MOMMO: His eyes now mild, lookin' straight ahead at nothing.

DOLLY: She's (MARY) gone loopey too.

MARY: Good girl.

MOMMO: Though 'twas polite introduction – 'How d'yeh do, Mr. Costello, I'm Seamus Ó'Toole'. Costello: 'Hah! I'm very well, thanking you!' His face was a study. An' 'Oh,' says John of Costello, 'He's a Sh-Sheamus too, phuh-phuh-phuh-phuh.' 'I know that,' says the stranger, 'but I'm a better laugher than 'm.' 'Kuhaa, uck-uck-uck-khuck, kuh-haa a haa!' In Costello's throat. In response didn't the stranger make serious chuckle. And in response to that didn't Costello roar out a laugh.

A silent 'Jesus' from DOLLY. *She decides to take off her coat and see what effect flaunting her pregnancy will have.*

MARY *speaking simultaneously.*

MARY (*silently with* MOMMO): Then loud as you please.

MOMMO: Then loud as you please says Costello: 'He says, he says, he says,' says he, 'he's a better.' (*She claps her mouth shut.*) An' that was far as he got. For in the suddenness of a discovery he found out that he was cross.
   'Ara phat?' says he – He was nimble? – The full size of him skippin' backwards an' forwards, the dancing antics of a boxing-man. An' lookin' 'bout at his supporters, now hushed an' on their marks, 'He says, he says, he says,' says he, 'he's a better laugher than me!'
   What! Sure they never heard the likes. Nor how on earth to deal with it.

An' the upset on their own man's face!
– Oh, they wor greatly taken 'back.
They wor. Oh they wor. An' not up to
disseration things wor lookin'
dangerous.

DOLLY: She's getting tired – the
creature.

MARY: Shhh!

DOLLY: Cheers!

MARY: Cheers – Things were looking
dangerous.

MOMMO: They were. Oh, they wor.

MARY: 'Ary give me (a) pint outa that."

MOMMO: Costello?

MARY *nods.*

Swivellin' an' near knockin' them wor
behind him. But then in retraction
comes wheelin' back 'round, the head
like a dunkey's flung up at the ceilin',
eyes like a bull-frog's near out the
sockets an' the big mouth threwn open.
But God bless us an' save us, all the
emission was (a) class of a rattle'd put
shame to a magpie.

MARY (*silently, excited*): Shame to a
magpie.

MOMMO: Now he was humbled, the big
head on him hangin', went back to his
corner, turned his back on all present –
The hump that was on him! Oh his
feelin's wor hurted. (*She yawns.*) Oh
ho hun-neo.

MARY: Aa no.

MOMMO (*insistent*): Oh ho hun-neo!

MARY: Don't be pretendin', you had a
little nap a while ago.

MOMMO: Put the sup of milk there for
me now for the night.

MARY: I'll get the milk later. And the
others. Mommo?

MOMMO: Lookin' wildly, one to the
other, from their giant to the stranger,
none knowin' what to do.

DOLLY (*getting the milk*): Let her settle
down.

MARY: But they were vexed.

MOMMO: An' they knew it?

MARY *nods agreement and
encouragement.*

Oh they knew they were cross. An'
strainin' towards the stranger like
mastiffs on chains, fit to tear him
asunder.

DOLLY: And I don't know if you've
noticed, Mary, but the turf out there
won't last the winter. (*Approaching
with the milk.*) Here we are! I'll see to
the turf.

MARY (*takes the milk from* DOLLY):
No milk.

DOLLY: What are you at?

MARY: No milk! (*She puts it away.*)

MOMMO: And even Josie! – the odd
one!

DOLLY (*to herself*): Jesus Josie!

MOMMO: That always stood aloof! Even
he was infected with the venom (*that*)
had entered, an' all of the floor was
'vailable round him he began to walk
circles screechin' 'Hackah!' at the
stranger.

DOLLY: I want to have a talk!

MARY: Later.

DOLLY: A plan, a proposition.

MARY: Later.

MOMMO: Pardon?

DOLLY: And I've a little problem of my
own.

MARY: I think I've noticed. Go on,
Mommo, no one is stopping you.

MOMMO: Where's the milk for the
night, Miss?

MARY: Then striding to the stranger –
Costello: 'Excuse me there now a
minute, Mister – '

DOLLY: Mary –

MARY: No! No! 'Excuse me there now a
minute now – '

MOMMO: Pardon?

MARY: 'But what did you say to me
there a minute ago?' (*Waits for a beat
to see if* MOMMO *will continue.*) . . .
'That you're a better laugher than me,
is it?' . . . 'Well, would you care to put
a small bet on it?'

MOMMO (*suspiciously, but childlike*):
How do you know that?

MARY: Oh, I was told. But I never heard all of the story.

MOMMO: Hah? . . . Ar shurrup (*shut up*) outa that.

MARY: 'Well would you care to put a small bet on it?' And 'No' saying the stranger going back to his wife. 'But you're challenging me, challenging me, challenging me, y'are!'

MOMMO: 'No' saying the stranger, ''twas only a notion,' his eyes on the floor. For why? Forseeing fatalistic danger. (MARY *nods solemnly*.) Then joined the two little smiles cross the width of his mouth which he gave up to the hero as evidence sincere that he was for abnegating. Can yeh go on?

MARY: No. (*Cajoling*.) Can you?

MOMMO: Well. Costello was for agreein'? An' for understandin'? But th' others wor all circlin', jostlin', an pushin' – Josie flailin' like a thrasher – eggin' for diversion. 'He is, he is, challe'gin' yeh, he is!' 'Up Bochtán, up Bochtán, Bochtán forever!' Putting confusion in the head of Costello again. But the stranger – a cute man – headin' for the door, gives (*the*) nod an' wink to Costello so he'd comprehend the better the excitation (*that*) is produced by the aberration of a notion. Then in the fullness of magistrature, 'Attention!' roaring Costello, 'Attention!' roaring he to declare his verdict was dismissal, an' decree that 'twas all over.

MARY: Yes?

MOMMO: An' 'twas.

MARY: Aa, you have more for me?

MOMMO (*childlike*): Have I?

MARY *nods.* MOMMO *thinking her own thoughts, then she shakes her head.*

MARY: A laughing competition there would be.

MOMMO (*absently*): A what?

DOLLY: She's exhausted.

MARY: She's not.

MOMMO: Where was I? . . . The jostlin' an' pushin' . . . (*Then her eyes searching the floor, in half-memory, lamenting trampled sweets.*) The sweets.

MARY: Here they are. (*The ones that* DOLLY *brought.*)

MOMMO: The sweets. (*Rejecting the sweets, her eyes still searching the floor.*) In the jostlin' an' pushin' . . . The sweets for her children trampled under their boots.

MARY: Here they are, under your pillow. Here.

MOMMO (*takes them absently*): Hahum?

DOLLY: Can't you see she's –

MARY: She's not.

MOMMO: Phuh: dust.

DOLLY: And you're worn out too, Mary.

MARY: But if Costello decreed 'twas all over, how did it start?

MOMMO: How did? The small stranger, I told yeh, goin' out to check the weather for as had been forecasted the thaw was settling in.

MARY: I see!

MOMMO: An' sure they could have got home.

MARY: Yes?

MOMMO: They could have got home. (*Brooding, growls; then:*) Costello could decree. All others could decree. (*Quiet anger.*) But what about the things had been vexin' *her* for years? No, a woman isn't stick or stone. The forty years an' more in the one bed together an' he to rise in the mornin' and not to give her a glance. An' so long it had been he had called her by first name, she'd near forgot it herself . . . Brigit . . . Hah? . . . An' so she thought he hated her . . . An' maybe he did. Like everything else . . . An'. (*Her head comes up, eyes fierce.*) Yis, yis-yis, he's challe'gin' ye, he is!' She gave it to the Bochtáns. And to her husband returning? – maybe he would recant, but she'd renege matters no longer. 'Och hona ho gus hah-haa' – she hated him too.

MARY *leans back; she has not heard this part of the story before.*

MARY: . . . And what happened then?

MOMMO: An' what happened then.

Tried to pacify her. (*Growls.*) But-there-was-none-would-assuage-her. An' what happened then, an' what happened then. 'Stand up then,' says Costello. They already standin'. 'Scath siar uaim' to the rest to clear back off the floor. The arena was ready.

MARY: And what happened then?

MOMMO: An' what happened then . . . Tired, tired.

MARY: Mommo?

MOMMO (*now regarding* MARY *with suspicion*): . . . Shthap! . . . (*To herself:*) Tired . . . What's your business here? . . . There are no newses here for anyone about anything. Heh heh heh heh!

DOLLY: It's ten to ten. So he'll hardly come now, so off with yeh to sleep. There's the good girl, and we'll hear your confession again tomorrow night. There, there now. (*To* MARY:) That was a new bit. There, there now. She's in bye-byes.

MARY (*quietly*): She's not.

DOLLY: She's asleep! Mommo! . . . She's asleep, it's ten to ten. Ten to ten, 1984, and I read it – how long ago was it? – that by 1984 we'd all be going on our holidays to the moon in *Woman's Own.*

MARY: She's not asleep.

DOLLY: I'm not arg'in' about it. She's – resting.

MARY: And I'm going to rouse her again in a minute. You were saying?

DOLLY (*stretching herself, flaunting her stomach*): And a telly would fit nicely over there.

MARY: A plan, a proposition, you have it all figured out?

DOLLY: And I'm sorry now I spent the money on the video. No one uses it. You'd make more use of it. It has a remote. (*In answer to* MARY's *query 'remote':*) Yeh know? (*holds in your hand*) – and – (*further demonstrates*) – control.

MARY: I have a video here already (*Mommo*). What's your plan?

DOLLY: Wait'll we have a drink. She's guilty.

MARY: Guilty of what?

DOLLY: I don't know.

MARY: Then why –

DOLLY: I'm not arg'in' with yeh. (*Offering to top up* MARY's *drink.*)

MARY: Why can't you ever finish a subject or talk straight? I don't want another drink.

DOLLY: I'm talking straight.

MARY: What's on your mind, Dolly? I'm up to you.

DOLLY: There's no one up to Dolly.

MARY: Tck!

DOLLY: I'm talkin' straight!

Another car passes by outside.

Traffic. The weekend-long meeting at the computer plant place. And all the men, busy, locked outside the fence.

MARY (*abrupt movement to the table*): On second thoughts. (*And pours lemonade into her glass.*)

DOLLY (*is a bit drunk now and getting drunker*): No, wait a minute.

MARY: What-are-you-saying, Dolly?

DOLLY: An' that's why she goes on like a gramophone. Guilty.

MARY: This is nonsense.

DOLLY: And so are you.

MARY: So am I!

DOLLY: An' you owe me a debt.

MARY: What do I owe you?

DOLLY: *And* she *had* to get married.

MARY (*to herself*): Impossible.

DOLLY: No! No! – Mary? No. Wait a minute –

MARY (*fingers to her forehead*): Dolly, I'm –

DOLLY: I'm talkin' straight.

MARY: Trying to get a grip of – Ahmm. I'm trying to find – ahmm. Get control of – ahmm. My life, Dolly.

DOLLY: Yes. You're trying to say, make head and tail of it all, talk straight, like myself. No, Mary, hold on! You told me one thing, I'll tell you another. D'yeh remember the pony-and-trap-Sunday-outings? I don't. But I remember – now try to contradict this – the day we buried Grandad. Now I was his favourite so I'll never forget it. And whereas – No, Mary! – whereas! She stood there over that hole in the ground like a rock – like a duck, like a duck, her chest stickin' out. Not a tear.

MARY: What good would tears have been?

DOLLY: Not a tear. And – *And!* – Tom buried in that same hole in the ground a couple of days before. Not a tear, then or since. (*Wandering to the table for another drink.*) Oh I gathered a few 'newses' about our Mommo.

MARY: Maybe she's crying now.

DOLLY: *All* of them had to get married except myself and Old Sharp Eyes. Mrs McGrath the sergeant said. But she bore a bastard all the same. Her Stephen. (*Wanders to the radio and switches it off.*) The hypocrite.

MARY: Leave it on.

DOLLY: I've a proposition.

MARY: It's the Sunday Concert. Switch it on.

DOLLY (*switches on the radio*): So what d'yeh think?

MARY: About what?

DOLLY: The slated (*gestures roof*), the other things I mentioned.

MARY: It would stop the place falling down for someone alright.

DOLLY: An' half of this place is mine, I'll sign it over.

MARY: To whom?

DOLLY: To whom. To Jack-Paddy-Andy, to Kitty-the-Hare, to you. And there might be – other things – you might need.

MARY: What else could anyone need?

DOLLY *now looking a bit hopeless, pathetic, offering a cigarette to* MARY, *lighting it for* MARY.

DOLLY: An' would you like another? (*drink*)

MARY *shakes her head.*

Lemonade?

MARY: No. What are you trying to say?

DOLLY: An' the turf out there won't last the winter.

MARY: You said that.

DOLLY: And one of the children.

She looks at MARY *for a reaction. But all this time* MARY's *mind, or half of it, is on* MOMMO.

Yeh. Company for yeh.

MARY: I get all this if I stay.

DOLLY: Or go.

MARY (*becoming more alert*): . . . What? . . . You want me to go? With one of the children? . . . *Which* one of the children?

DOLLY (*continues with closed eyes through the following*): Jesus, I'm tired. A brand new one.

MARY *laughs incredulously.*

Would you? Would you? Would you?

MARY: What?

DOLLY: Take him. It.

MARY: With me?

DOLLY (*nods*): An' no one need be any the wiser.

MARY: And if I stay?

DOLLY: Say it's yours. It'll all blow over in a month.

MARY: You're crazy.

DOLLY: That makes three of us. I'm not crazy. I'm – as you can see.

MARY: Yes, I've wondered for some time, but I thought you couldn't – you couldn't! – be that stupid.

A car passes by outside.

DOLLY: More take-aways for the lads. (*She starts wearily for her coat.*) My, but they're busy.

MARY: No one is asking you to leave.

DOLLY (*stops. Eyes closed again*): You'll be paid.

MARY: I've heard you come up with a few things before, but!

DOLLY: Stephen'll kill me.

MARY: What about me?

DOLLY: Or he'll cripple me.

MARY: Do you ever think of others!

DOLLY: Or I'll fix him.

MARY: And you'll be out – gallivanting – again tomorrow night.

DOLLY: And the night after, and the night after. And you can be sure of that.

MARY: How long are you gone?

DOLLY: Six, seven months.

MARY: Six, seven months.

DOLLY: Trying to conceal it.

MARY: Who's the father?

DOLLY: I have my suspicions.

MARY: But he's busy perhaps tonight, picketing?

DOLLY: Yes, very busy. Travelling at the sound of speed. But the Chinese'll get them. (*Opens her eyes.*) Hmm?

MARY: And this is the help? This is what you've been figuring out?

DOLLY: You can return the child after, say, a year. If you want to.

MARY: I thought your figuring things out were about –? (*She indicates* MOMMO. *Then she goes to* MOMMO.) Mommo, open your eyes, time to continue.

DOLLY: After a year it'll be easy to make up a story.

MARY: *Another* story! (*She laughs.*)

DOLLY: You're a nurse, you could help me if you wanted to.

MARY: Trying all my life to get out of *this* situation and now you want to present me with the muddle of your stupid life to make *sure* the saga goes on.

DOLLY: Oh the saga will go on.

MARY: Mommo!

DOLLY: I'll see to that, one way or the other.

MARY (*to herself*): I go away with a brand new baby. Mommo! (*To* DOLLY:) Where! Where do I go?

DOLLY *nods.*

You have that figured out too?

DOLLY: We can discuss that.

MARY *laughs.*

You're its aunt.

MARY: Its! (*She laughs.*)

DOLLY: Aunt! – Aunt! – And you're a nurse! – Aunt!

MARY: Mommo! I know you're not asleep.

DOLLY (*shrugs*): OK. (*Now talking to herself:*) And if it's a boy you can call it Tom, and if it's a girl you can call it Tom. (*Continues talking through the following, wandering to the fire and sitting there. Dolly's speech, though to herself, dominating.*)

MOMMO: Supa milk, where's the milk?

MARY: Later.

MOMMO: Miss!

MARY: We're going to finish your nice story. Now! To continue. Where had you got to? Costello clearing his throat.

MOMMO: But in the jostlin' an' pushin' (*Eyes searching the floor.*) The sweets . . . the sweets . . .

DOLLY (*through the above*): But I've discussed something with someone. 'Cause if I don't get him he'll get me. But I know now how to get him and that's what got me saving, of late. I've made the preliminary enquiries. That little service of fixing someone is available – 'cause it's in demand – even round here. I've discussed it with someone.

MOMMO: The sweets.

MARY (*to* DOLLY): Have you finished?

DOLLY (*intensely*): You had it easy!

MARY: I had it easy? No one who came out of this – house – had it easy. (*To herself:*) I had it easy.

DOLLY: You-had-it-easy. The bright one, top of your class!

MARY (*to herself*): What would you know about it?

DOLLY: Top marks! – Hardly had your Leaving Cert. and you couldn't wait to be gone.

MARY: I won't deny that.

DOLLY: You can't! State Registered Nurse before you were twenty –

MARY: Twenty-one –

DOLLY: A Sister before you were twenty-five, Assistant Matron at the age of thirty.

MARY: And a midwife.

DOLLY: Yes, SRN, CMB, DDT.!

MARY: All very easy.

DOLLY: Couldn't get away fast enough.

MARY: But I came back, Dolly.

DOLLY: Aren't you great?

MARY: I failed. It all failed. I'm as big a failure as you, and that's some failure.

DOLLY *is stopped for a moment by* MARY's *admission.*

You hadn't considered that?

MOMMO *has started rambling again, repeating the last section of the story which she told earlier, down to 'The arena was ready'.*

MOMMO: An' sure they could have got home. An' the small stranger, her husband sure, was goin' out to check the weather, for as had been forecasted the thaw was . . .

DOLLY (*her voice over* MOMMO's): No! No! You had it easy! – You had it – You had – I had – I had ten! – I had a lifetime! – A lifetime! – Here with herself, doin' her every bidding, listenin' to her seafóid (*rambling*) gettin' worse till I didn't know where I was! – Pissin' in the bed beside me – I had a lifetime! Then the great Stephen – the surprise of it! comes coortin'! Never once felt any – real – warmth from him – what's wrong with him? – but he's my rescuer, my saviour. But then, no rhyme or reason to it – He could've got a job at that plant, but he couldn't wait to be gone either! Then waitin' for the hero, my rescuer, the sun shining out of his eighty-five-pounds-a-week arse, to come home at Christmas. No interest in me – oh, he used me! – or in children, or the rotten thatch or the broken window, or Conor above moving in his fence from *this* side. I'm fightin' all the battles. Still

fightin' the battles. And what d'yeh think he's doin' now this minute? Sittin' by the hearth in Coventry, is he? Last Christmas an' he was hardly off the bus, Old Sharp Eyes whisperin' into his ear about me. Oooo, but he waited. Jesus, how I hate him! Jesus, how I hate them! Men! Had his fun and games with me that night, *and* first thing in the morning. Even sat down to eat the hearty breakfast I made. Me thinkin', still no warmth, but maybe it's goin' to be okay. Oooo, but I should've known from *experience* about-the-great-up-stand-in'-Steph-en-evrabody's-fav-our-ite. Because, next thing he has me by the hair of the head, fistin' me down in the mouth, Old Sharp Eyes there, noddin' her head every time he struck an' struck an' kicked an' kicked an' pulled me round the house by the hair of the head. Jesus, men! (*Indicating the outdoors where she had her sex.*) You-think-I-enjoy? I-use-*them*! Jesus, hypocrisy! An' then, me left with my face like a balloon – you saw a lot of me last Christmas, didn't yeh? – my body black and blue, the street angel an' his religious mother – 'As true as Our Lady is in heaven now, darlin's' – over the road to visit you an' Mommo with a little present an' a happy an' a holy Christmas now darlin's an' blessed St-fuckin'-Jude an' all the rest of them flyin' about for themselves up there.

MOMMO: The arena was ready. A laughing competition there would be. (*She coughs in preparation.*)

DOLLY (*at* MOMMO): Och hona ho gus hah-haa! Jesus, how I hate them! I hate her (*Mommo*) – I hate this house – She hates you – I hate my own new liquorice-all-sorts-coloured house –

MARY, DOLLY *speaking simultaneously:*

MARY (*ashen-face, shaking her head*): No . . . No.

DOLLY: She! – She! – She hates you.

MARY: No.

MOMMO, DOLLY *speaking simultaneously:*

MOMMO: 'Wuff a wuff! A wuha wuha wuha wuha, wock-ock och ock och och ock – Naaw.'

DOLLY: And I hate you.

MARY: Why?

DOLLY: Why.

MOMMO: 'Heh heh heh heh,' proud, aisy an' gentle.

DOLLY: You don't know terror, you don't know hatred, you don't know desperation

MOMMO: An' sure Costello's laughin' wasn't right at all.

DOLLY: No one came out of this house had it easy but you had it easy.

MOMMO: 'Quock uck-uck-uck-uck quock?' (MOMMO unwrapping a sweet and putting it in her mouth.)

MARY: Dolly, stop it at once!

DOLLY:'Dolly, stop it at once.' Look, go away an' stay away.

MARY: Dolly –

MOMMO: 'Heh heh heh heh heh.'

DOLLY: 'This is our home' – You'll need a few bob, I'll give it to you, and my grand plan: I'll look after things here, all fronts, including lovee lovee Mommo, an' Stephen'll never raise a finger to me again.

MARY: You're –

DOLLY: Am I?

MARY: You're –

DOLLY: Am I? We'll see – Hah! – if I'm bluffing.

MARY: Have you finished ranting?

DOLLY: Ooh, ranting!

MOMMO (looking at the floor): The sweets . . . the sweets (Whispering.)

MARY: You're spoilt, you're unhappy, you're running round in circles.

DOLLY: I'm running round in circles? Suitcase packed – How many times? Puttin' on airs – look at the boots, look at the lady! You're stayin', you're goin', 'I need to talk to someone' – Fuck off! 'I wanted to come home, I had to come home' – Fuck off!

MARY: Stop it this moment, I won't have it! You're frightening her.

In reply to 'frightening her', DOLLY indicates MOMMO who is now sucking a sweet, lost in her own thoughts. Then DOLLY turns to look into the fire, her back to MARY; she continues in quieter tone.

DOLLY: The countryside produced a few sensations in the last couple of years, but my grand plan: I'll show them what can happen in the dark of night in a field. I'll come to grips with my life.

Short silence.

MOMMO's eyes fixed on MARY.

MOMMO: Miss! . . . Do I know you?

MARY shakes her head, 'No': she is afraid to speak: if she does she will cry. . . . Pardon?

MARY shakes her head.

DOLLY (to the fire): I'll finish another part of this family's history in grander style than any of the others.

MARY: . . . The arena was ready.

MOMMO: 'Twas.

MARY: But Costello's laugh wasn't right at all.

MOMMO: Then ''Scuse me a minute,' says he lickin' his big mouth, puts a spit in the one hand, then one in the other, an' ponderin' the third that he sent to the floor. (Coughs.) 'A wuff.'

DOLLY: A wuff, wuff!

MOMMO: 'A wuha wuha wuha wuha, a wuha huha huha hoo, quock-uckina na hoona ho ho, a wo ho ho ho ho ho ho!' An' twasn't bad at all. Was it? An' Costello knew it. An' by way of exper'ment, though 'twasn't his turn, had a go at it again, his ear cocked to himself.

DOLLY: Heh heh heh heh heh heh heh – We filled half that graveyard.

MOMMO: We did. But then, ''Scuse me too,' says the stranger makin' Costello stiffen, an' 'Heh heh heh, heh heh heh, heh heh heh,' chuckled he.

DOLLY: Heh heh heh, heh heh heh, heh heh heh – Well, I'll fill the other half.

MARY (ferociously at DOLLY): Shthap!

DOLLY: Och hona ho gus hah-haa!

MOMMO: Pardon?

MARY (to MOMMO): . . . No, you don't know me. But I was here once, and I ran away to try and blot out here. I didn't have it easy. Then I tried bad things, for a time, with someone. So I came back, thinking I'd find – something – here, or, if I didn't, I'd put everything right. Mommo? And tonight I thought I'd make a last try. Live out the – story – finish it, move on to a place where, perhaps, we could make some kind of new start. I want to help you.

DOLLY: And yourself.

MARY: And myself. Mommo?

MOMMO: Where's the milk for the night?

MARY nods that she will get it.

MOMMO: Tck!

MARY (gently to DOLLY): She may hate me, you may hate me. But I don't hate her. I love her for what she's been through, and she's all that I have. So she has to be my only consideration. She doesn't understand. Do you understand, Dolly? Please . . . And I'm sorry.

DOLLY (drunkenly): For what?

MARY (turns away tearfully): I'm not the saint you think I am.

DOLLY: The what? Saint? That'd be an awful thing to be. 'Wo ho ho, ho ho ho!'

MARY puts the milk by the bed.

MOMMO: Yis. Did yeh hear? The full style was returnin' – 'Wo ho ho, wo ho ho!' An' like a great archbishop turnin' on his axis, nods an' winks to his minions that he knew all along. The cheers that went up in John Mah'ny's that night!
  An' now what did they start doin', the two gladiators, circlin' the floor, eyes riveted together, silent in quietude to find the advantage, save the odd whoop from Costello, his fist through the ceilin', an' the small little stranger'd bate the odd little dance. Now! Then. And.
  'Yeh sold all your cargo?' Costello roarin' like a master to friken a

scholar. The laugh from his attendants, but then so did the stranger.
  'Where (are) yeh bound for?' – stern Costello – 'Your destination, a Mhico?'
  'Ballindineside, your worship.'
  'Ballindineside, a Thighearna!'

DOLLY: Oh ho ho, wo ho ho.

MOMMO: 'Cunn ether iss syha soory.' (Coinn iotair is saidhthe suaraighe)

DOLLY: Hounds of rage and bitches of wickedness!

MOMMO: An' the description despicable more fitting their own place.

DOLLY (to the fire, almost dreamily): Why the fuck did he marry me?

It only lasts a second, but MARY holds a glance on the now pathetic-looking DOLLY.

MOMMO: 'A farmer?' says Costello. 'A goose one,' says the stranger. An' t'be fair to the Bochtáns they plauded the self-denigration.

DOLLY: I don't hate anyone.

MOMMO: 'An' yourself?' says the stranger. 'Oh now you're questionin' me,' says Costello. 'An' Rabbits,' screeches Josie, 'Hull-hull-hull, hull-hull-hull!'

DOLLY (stands): What did I get up for?

MARY and DOLLY forget themselves and start laughing at MOMMO's dramatisation of this section.

MOMMO: An', 'Rabbits!' says the stranger. 'Rabbits!' says he, 'heh – heh.' 'Well, heh heh heh, heh heh heh, heh heh heh, heh heh heh!' 'What's the cause of your laughter?' Costello frownin' moroya. (Mar dhea; pretending seriousness) 'Bunny rabbits! says the stranger – 'is that what you're in!'

MARY and DOLLY laughing their own laughter.

'Not at all, me little man,' says Costello, 'I've a herd of trinamanooses in Closh back the road.'
  'Tame ones?' says the stranger.
  'Tame ones, what else, of a certainty,' says Costello, 'An' the finest breed for 'atin' sure!'
  'But for the Townies though for

'atin',' says the stranger most sincerely. 'An not able to keep the straight face, Costello roared out a laughter an' gave beck to his attendants to plaud the stranger's cleverality.

The three of them laughing.

Now wasn't he able for them?

DOLLY: Where's the flashlamp?

MOMMO: An' the contrariety an' venom was in it while ago!

DOLLY: I want to go out the back.

MARY: It's on top of the dresser.

MOMMO: But now they couldn't do enough for that decent man an' woman, all vying with each other – an' sure they didn't have it – to buy treats for the strangers. Tumblers of whiskey an' bumpers of port wine. A strange auld world right enough. But in some wisdom of his own he made it this way. 'Twas the nicest night ever.

DOLLY (*has got the flashlamp; a plea in her voice*): Mary?

MARY: 'Twas the nicest night ever.

MOMMO: But they'd yet to find the topic would keep them laughin' near forever.

DOLLY: Mary?

MARY: Topic?

MOMMO: Then one'd laugh solo, the other'd return, then Costello'd go winkin' an' they'd both laugh together, a nod from the stranger (*and*) they'd stop that same moment to urge riotous chorus, give the others a chance.

DOLLY: Don't want the fuggin' flashlamp. (*She discards it. Then, as if driving cattle out of the house, she goes out the back door.*) How! – How! – How! Hup! – Skelong! – Bleddy cows! Howa-that-how! – Hup! Hup!

MARY: What topic did they find?

MOMMO: But there can be no gainsayin' it, Costello clear had the quality laugh. 'Wo ho ho, ho ho ho' (in) the barrel of his chest would great rumbles start risin', the rich rolls of round sound out of his mouth, to explode in the air an' echo back rev'berations. The next time demonstratin' the range of his skill, go

flyin' aloft (to) the heights of registration – 'Hickle-ickle-ickle-ickle!' – like a hen runnin' demented from the ardent attentions, over-persistent, of a cock in the yard after his business. Now!

MARY: What about Grandad?

MOMMO: Who?

MARY: The stranger.

MOMMO: Not much by way of big sound?

MARY: No.

MOMMO: Or rebounding modulation?

MARY: No.

MOMMO: But was that a stipulation?

MARY: No.

MOMMO: He knew the tricks of providence and was cunning of exertion. Scorn for his style betimes?

MARY *nods.*

But them wor his tactics.

MARY: And he was most in control.

MOMMO: He was. (*She yawns.*) Tired.

MARY: No. Mommo. It *is* a nice story. And you've nearly told it all tonight. Except for the last picece that you never tell. Hmm?

MOMMO: Who was that woman?

MARY: What woman?

MOMMO: Tck! – That woman just went out the door there. (*Mimicking DOLLY:*) 'Hup-hup-howa that'?

MARY: That was Dolly . . . Dolly.

MOMMO: An' does she always behave that way?

MARY: Sometimes.

MOMMO (*thinking about this: it does not make sense to her. Then eyes scrutinising MARY: in this moment she is possibly close to recognising MARY*): . . . Who are (*you*)?

MARY: Try a guess. Yes, Mommo? – Yes, Mommo? – Please – who am I?

MOMMO: Here she is again!

DOLLY *comes in. She looks bloated and tired. She wolfs down the slice of cake which she deliberately resisted earlier. Then looking for her bag, putting on her overcoat, etc.*

DOLLY: And I've been starving myself.

MOMMO (*whispering*): She'd eat yeh out of house an' home . . . Is there something you require, Miss, that you're rummaging for over there?

DOLLY (*realises she is being spoken to*): Your pension.

MOMMO: Oh it's time for ye both to be going – ten to ten. He doesn't like calling when there's strangers in the house.

MARY: We're off now in a minute. What was that topic again that kept them on laughing?

MOMMO: Misfortunes. (*She yawns.*)

MARY: Mommo? (MOMMO's *eyes are closed.*)

DOLLY (*to herself, looking at the door*): I hate going home.

MARY: Mommo? Or if you like the bit about 'Out of the bushes more of them was comin'.'

MOMMO: Tom is in Galway. (*Opens her eyes.*) I bet him with nettles. Mitchin' from school. D'yeh think he remembers?

MARY (*gently*): No.

MOMMO (*closes her eyes*): Well, I don't remember . . . I don't remember any more of it.

MARY (*tired, futile*): And out of the bushes more of them was comin'?

MOMMO (*drowsily*): I don't remember any more of it.

MARY: Wherever their hovels were, holes in the ground . . . 'cause 'twas place of desolation.

DOLLY (*another plea*): Mary?

MARY (*eyes continue on* MOMMO *who is now asleeep*): Sit down.

DOLLY *remains standing, wondering is there hope for her in* MARY's *remark.*

DOLLY: . . . What were you trying to do with her?

MARY: 'Twas only a notion . . . She's asleep.

DOLLY: . . . Maybe she'd wake up again?

MARY (*slight shake of her head, 'No'*): Sit down?

DOLLY (*sits*): . . . What're yeh goin' to do?

MARY (*slight shake of her head, a tremulous sigh*): Ahmm.

DOLLY: . . . Back to the nursing?

Slight shake of the head from MARY.

. . . What?

MARY: No. That wasn't me at all. And no confidence now anyway. (*She collects up a few odds and ends and puts them in the suitcase.*) Who's looking after the children?

DOLLY: Maisie Kelly. They're stayin' the night in her house. She knows. She said if I had to go away for a day or anything . . . I don't want to go away.

MARY (*absently*): The nicest night ever.

DOLLY: . . . What were we doin' that night?

MARY: Ahmm. The shade on that light: do you mind if I? (*She switches off the light and lights a candle.*) We let the fire go out. The cursèd paraffin.

MARY *has collected up a silver-backed hairbrush and a clothes brush.*

DOLLY: . . . But if you're not going back to the nursing?

MARY: There must be *something*, some future for me, somewhere. (*She is brushing the back of* DOLLY's *coat.*) I can certainly scrub floors.

DOLLY (*a little irritably*): What're you doin'?

MARY: Just a little – dust – here.

DOLLY: Who cares?

MARY: It's just that people talk at the slightest.

DOLLY: Na bac na ciaróigí (*ciaróga*). (*Don't mind the gossipers*)

MARY: When I was a nurse there was a patient, terminal, an elderly woman and we became very close.

DOLLY: Do you care what people say?

MARY: I'm afraid I do. There. (*The coat is brushed; she now brushes* DOLLY'*s hair.*) I don't know why she used to watch me or why she chose to make friends with me.

DOLLY: What are you doin' now?

MARY: But one day she said, in the middle of – whatever – conversations we were having, 'You're going to be alright, Mary.' Simple remark. But it took me by surprise. Like, a *promised* blessing. And why I should have – (*Shrugs.*) believed in it for, oh twenty years? until recently, I don't know. There. (DOLLY'*s hair is brushed.*) She left me these (*the brushes*) and this (*the teapot*) and the book. (*She dumps the lot into the suitcase.*)

DOLLY: If I sat down to write a book.

MARY: Though the book has always depressed me a bit. *Winter Words.* I can't do a thing for you, Dolly. Can you lend me a hundred quid?

DOLLY *nods.*

Well, that's it then.

DOLLY *is just sitting there looking into the fire;* MARY *standing, her back to the suitcase, her hands resting on it: two figures frozen in time. Then the cortège of cars approaching, passing the house (at comparatively slow speed).*

DOLLY: The funeral. The weekend-long meeting is over. Now are they travelling at the sound of speed?

MARY *laughs.*

I told you the Chinese'd get them. (*They are beginning to laugh. looking at her stomach – the bulge.*) Good man Josie!

MARY *laughs.* DOLLY *joins in the laughter.* DOLLY *flaunting herself, clowning:*

And you're his aunt!

They laugh louder; the laughter getting out of hand.

(*To her stomach*): Good man Josie! . . . (*Uproariously;*) Jesus, misfortunes!

Then the unexpected, MOMMO'*s voice.*

MOMMO: Scoth caoc!

Silence.

What time is it?

MARY: Seven! (*In a whisper, waiting, frozen.*)

MOMMO: Explosions of laughter an' shouts of hurrahs!

DOLLY (*sits heavily on the bed*): Jesus, I'm tired.

MARY (*pleading with* DOLLY): Dolly!

MOMMO: For excess of joy.

DOLLY: 'S alright, 'salright, Mommo: I'm Dolly, I'm like a film star. (*To* MARY:) 'S alright.

MOMMO: An' didn't he ferret out her eyes to see how she was farin', an' wasn't she titherin' with the best of them an' weltin' her thighs. No heed on her now to be gettin' on home. No. But offerin' to herself her own congratulations at hearin' herself laughin'. An' then, like a girl, smiled at her husband, an' his smile back so shy, like the boy he was in youth. An' the moment was for them alone. Unawares of all cares, unawares of all the others. An' how long before since their eyes had met, mar gheal dhá gréine, glistenin' for each other. Not since long and long ago.

And now Costello's big hand was up for to call a recession. 'But how,' says he, 'is it to be indisputably decided who is the winner?' And a great silence followed. None was forgettin' this was a contest. An' the eyes that wor dancin', now pending the answer, glazed an' grave in dilation: 'Twas a difficult question. (*Quietly:*) Och-caw. Tired of waiting male intelligence, 'He who laughs last' says she.

An' 'cause 'twas a woman that spoke it, I think Costello was frikened, darts class of a glance at her an' – (*She gulps.*) 'That's what I thought,' says he. But wasn't that his mistake? ever callin' the recession an' he in full flight. 'Cause now, ready himself as he would, with his coughin' an' spittin', the sound emanating from a man of his talent, so forced and ungracious, he'd stop it himself.

(*Whispering.*) 'He's lost it,' says someone. Och hona ho gus hah-haa! (*Whispering.*) 'He should never have stopped.' Their faces like mice. An' he'd 'tempt it an' 'tempt it an' 'tempt it again. Ach an fear mór as Bochtán (*But the big man from Bochtán*) in respiratory disaster is i ngreas casachtaí (*and in bouts of coughing*). (*She coughs . . .*) The contest was over.

MARY: The contest was over?

MOMMO: 'Twas.

MARY: The contest was over?

MOMMO: The contest was over. Oh the strangers'd won.

MARY: But what about the topic?

MOMMO: Hah?

MARY: Would keep them laughing near forever.

MOMMO (*whispers*): Misfortunes . . . *She* supplied them with the topic. And it started up again with the subject of potatoes, the damnedable crop was in it that year.
    'Wet an' wat'rey?' says the stranger.
    'Wet an' wat'rey,' laughing Costello.
    'Heh heh heh, but not blighted?'
    'No ho ho, ho ho ho, but scabby an' small.'
    'Sour an' soapy – Heh heh heh.'
    'Yis – ho ho,' says the hero. 'Hard to wash, ladies? Hard to boil, ladies?'
    'An' the divil t'ate – Heh heh heh!'
But they were only getting into their stride.
    'An' the hay?' says old Brian, 'behell.'
    'Rotted!' says the contestants, roarin' it together.
    'The bita oats,' shouts young Kemple – 'Jasus!' Lodged in the field. An' the turf says another. Still in the bog, laughed the answer. An' the chickens the pip, pipes up the old crone. An' the sheep, the staggers. An' the cow that just died. An' the man that was in it lost both arms to the thresher. An' the *dead!*

MARY: . . . And the dead, Mommo?

MOMMO (*whimpers*): I wanta see mah father.

MARY: Who were the dead?

MOMMO: Pardon? Skitherin' an' laughin' – Hih-hih-hih – at their nearest an' dearest. Her Pat was her eldest, died of consumption, had his pick of the girls an' married the widdy again'

all her wishes. The decline in that fambly, she knew the widdy'd outlast him. She told them the story – Hih-hih-hih – an' many another. An' how Pat, when he came back for the two sheep (*that*) wor his – An' they wor – An' he was her first-born. But you'll not have them she told him. Soft Willie inside, quiet by the hearth, but she knew he'd be able, the spawgs of hands he had on him. 'Is it goin' fightin' me own brother?' But she told him a brother was one thing, but she was his mother, an' them were the orders to give Pat the high road, and no sheep one, two or three was leavin' the yard. They hurted each other. An' how Pat went back empty to his strap of a widdy. An' was dead within a six months. Hih-hih-hih. (*The 'hih-hih-hih' which punctuate her story sounds more like tears – ingrown sobs – rather than laughter.*) Oh she made great contribution to the rollcall of the dead. Was she what or 'toxicated? An' for the sake of an auld ewe was stuck in the flood was how she lost two of the others, Jimmy and Michael. Great gales of laughter to follow each name of the departed. Hih-hih-hih. An' the nice wife was near her time, which one of them left behind him?

MARY: Daddy.

MOMMO: Died tryin' to give birth to the fourth was to be in it. An' she herself left with the care of three small childre waitin'. All contributions receiving volleys of cheers. Nothin' was sacred an' nothing a secret. The unbaptised an' stillborn in shoeboxes planted, at the dead hour of night treading softly the Lisheen to make the regulation hole – not more, not less than two feet deep – too fearful of the field, haunted by infants, to speak or to pray. They were fearful of their ankles – Hih-hih-hih. An' tryin' not to hasten, steal away again, leaving their pagan parcels in isolation forever. Hih-hih-hih. Her soft Willie was her pet went foreign after the others. An' *did* she drive them all away? Never ever to be heard of, ever again: Save soft Willie, aged thirty-four, in Louisaville Kentucky, died, peritonites. Spell that. A-N-T Yes? I-P-H- Yes? F-U-L- Yes? L-O-G- Yes? E-S-T- Yes? I-N-E-

Antiphfullogestine. Now! That's how I taught them all to spell. Hih-hih-hih! The nicest night they ever had, that's what I'm sayin'. The stories kept on comin' an' the volleys and cheers. All of them present, their heads threwn back abandoned in festivities of guffaws: the wretched and neglected dilapidated an' forlorn, the forgotten an' tormented, the lonely an' despairing, ragged an' dirty, impoverished, hungry, emaciated and unhealthy, eyes big as saucers ridiculing an' defying of their lot on earth below – glintin' their defiance – their defiance an' rejection, inviting of what else might come or care to come! – driving bellows of refusal at the sky through the roof. Och hona ho gus hah-haa! . . . The nicest night ever.

MARY: An' what else was to come?

MOMMO: Nothing.

MARY: Tom.

MOMMO: Tom is in Galway.

MARY: Grandad.

MOMMO: An' when I told me father what did he say? ''Twas a *double* insolence at heaven.' We weren't meant to be here at all! 'Making mock of God's prize piece, its structure and system.' 'Oh,' he groaned, 'I have wrestled with enigmals (*all*) my life-long years. I've combed all of creation,' that man intoned, 'and, in the wondrous handiwork of God, have found only two flaws, man an' the earwig. Of what use is man, what utility the earwig, where do they either fit in the system? They are both specimens desperate, without any control, and therefore unfree. One cocks his head,' says he, 'the other his tail. But God will not be mocked. Especially when He was so clever at creating all things else. Still, God must have said, I'll leave them there an' see what transpires.' An' says me father – (*She winks shrewdly.*) 'Maybe the earwig isn't doin' too bad at all.' An' then he tied his hands.

MARY: Who did?

MOMMO: Tck! Me father. That 'twas a double insolence at heaven. But they'd soon get their answer.

MARY: Who would?

MOMMO: The Bochtáns, the Bochtáns sure! Tck! Mauleogs drunk?

MARY *nods.*

Them all packed together?

MARY *nods.*

The foul odour that was in it, you'd hardly get your breath. The ache was in the laughter. The two contestants sweating, the big man most profusely. Sure they'd been contending the title now for five or six hours. An' Costello, openin' down his shirts an' loosenin' his buckle, was doublin' up an' staggerin' an' holdin' his sides. 'Aw Jasus, lads, ye have me killed – Hickle-ickle-ickle,' an' the laughing lines upon his mien wor more like lines of pain. An' the stranger goin' 'Heh heh heh heh, heh heh heh heh.' Aisy an' gentle. Then beholding his 'ponent from contortion to convulsion, his complexion changin' colours an' arrivin' at purple: 'Heh heh heh heh, heh heh . . . heh . . . heh . . . heh,' the frown to his brow bringin' stillness upon him an' the two little smiles to the sides of his mouth. Suddenly he shouts, 'Costello's the winner!' But sure they wouldn't have it – nor herself in the corner. 'He's nat (*not*), he's nat, he's nat, he's nat!' 'On, on-on, Bochtán forever!'
   'No-no! – Heh heh – he has me bet!'
   'He's nat, he's nat, he's nat, he's nat!'
   The others, 'Up Bochtán – On Bochtán! Bochtán forever!'
   An Costello now all the while in upper registration – 'Hickle-ickle-ickle-ickle' – longin' to put stop to it, his own cacklin' wouldn't let him. An' 'deed, when he'd 'tempt to rise an arm – an' sure he wasn't able – in gesture of cessation, th' other mistakin' of his purpose would go thinkin' t' do it for'm (*for him*) puncturin' holes in the ceilin', batin' stomps on the floor.
   An' the stranger now could only stand and watch. An' late it was herself realised the Great Adversary had entered.
   'Hickle-ickle-ickle-ickle – Aw Jasus, lads, I'm dyin', – Oh not without effort. Hickle, ickle, ickle, ickle. Then

slow in a swoon he went down to the floor. For the last moments were left him 'twas the stranger that held him, for there was nothing in the world to save him, or able to save him. Now!

MARY: And what's the rest of it?

MOMMO: Pardon?

MARY: For there was nothing now in the world. Only a little bit left.

MOMMO (*musing*): For there was nothing now in the world . . .

DOLLY *is stirring in her sleep and wakes up for a moment.*

DOLLY: Mary?

MARY (*regards her gravely for a moment; then*): . . . You're going to be alright, Dolly. Roll in under the blanket.

DOLLY *goes back to sleep.*

MOMMO: To save him . . . Or able to save him. Did I not say that? Oh yis. 'An' the rabbits, lads,' says Cost'llo, 'I didn't sell e'er the one of them, but threwn them comin' home for fun again' Patch Curran's door.' And that was the last he was to utter that night or any other.

MARY: They don't laugh there anymore.

MOMMO: Save the childre, until they arrive at the age of reason. Now! Bochtán forever is Bailegangaire.

Through the following MARY *undresses behind the headboard and puts on her long simple nightdress; she lets down her hair, gets the hairbrush from the case and brushes her hair. Switches off the radio. She looks remarkably beautiful: she is like a young elegant woman, her face introspective and grave.*

MARY: To conclude.

MOMMO: To conclude. The thaw as was forecasted was in it, an' the strangers went home.

MARY: But didn't they hurt grandad? . . . The stranger, his ribs?

MOMMO: They did. But he bet them – he bet the best of them.

MARY: And wasn't his face cut?

MOMMO: Oh they did. They did. They

wor for lettin' them home. D'yeh know? Home without hinder. Till the thief, Josie, started cryin', cryin' at death, and was insistently demanding the boots be took of the stranger to affirm 'twas feet or no was in them. An' from trying to quieten his gathering excitation someone of them got hit. Then he struck back. Till they forgot what they wor doin' sure, or how it had started, but all drawin' kicks an' blows, one upon the other, till the venom went rampant. They pulled him down off the cart an' gave him the kickin'. They did. Oh they gave him such a doin', till John Mah'ny an' the curate (*that*) was called prevailed again' the Bolsheviks.

MARY *gets into bed beside* MOMMO. DOLLY *is asleep on the other side.*

'Twas dawn when they got home. Not without trepidation? But the three small childre, like ye, their care, wor safe an' sound fast asleep on the settle. Now, my fondlings, settle down an' be sayin' yere prayers. I forget what happened the three sticks of rock. Hail Holy Queen. Yes? Mother of Mercy. Yes? Hail our lives? Yes? Our sweetness and our hope.

MARY: It was a bad year for the crops, a good one for mushrooms, and the three small children were waiting for their gran and their grandad to come home. Mommo? My bit. Mary was the eldest. She was the clever one, and she was seven. Dolly, the second, was like a film-star and she was grandad's favourite. And they were in and out of the road watching for the horse and cart. Waiting for ribbons. And Tom who was the youngest, when he got excited would go pacing o'er and o'er the boundary of the yard. He had confided in Mary his expectation. They would be bringing him his dearest wish – grandad told him secretly – that was alright. But in the – excitation – of their waiting they forgot to pay attention to the fire. Then Mary and Dolly heard – 'twas like an explosion. Tom had got the paraffin and, not the way grandad did it, sthelled it on to the embers, and the sudden blaze came out on top of him. And when they ran in and . . .

saw him, Mary got . . . hysterical. And Dolly following suit got the same. Then Mary sent Dolly across the fields for May Glynn. And sure May was only . . . eleven? Then Mary covered . . . the wounds . . . from the bag of flour in the corner. She'd be better now, and quicker now, at knowing what to do. And then May Glynn's mother came and they took Tom away to Galway, where he died . . . Two mornings later, and he had only just put the kettle on the hook, didn't grandad, the stranger, go down too, slow in a swoon . . . Mommo?

MOMMO: It got him at last.

MARY: Will you take your pills now?

MOMMO: The yellow ones.

MARY: Yes.

MOMMO: Poor Séamus.

MOMMO *takes the pills with a sup of milk. Or, perhaps it is now that* MARY *gets into the bed.*

MARY: Is there anything else you need?

MOMMO: To thee do we cry. Yes? Poor banished children of Eve.

MARY: Is there anything you have to say to me?

MOMMO: Be sayin' yere prayers now an' ye'll be goin' to sleep. To thee do we send up our sighs. Yes? For yere Mammy an' Daddy an' grandad is (*who are*) in heaven.

MARY: And Tom.

MOMMO: Yes. An' he only a ladeen was afeared of the gander. An' tell them ye're all good. Mourning and weeping in this valley of tears. (*She is handing the cup back to* MARY, *her eyes held on* MARY.) And sure a tear isn't such a bad thing, Mary, and haven't we everything we need here, the two of us. (*And she settles down to sleep.*)

MARY (*tears of gratitude brim to her eyes; fervently*): Oh we have, Mommo.

Her tears continue to the end but her crying is infused with a sound like the laughter of relief.

. . . To conclude. It's a strange old place alright, in whatever wisdom He has to have made it this way. But in whatever wisdom there is, in the year 1984, it was decided to give that – fambly . . . of strangers another chance, and a brand new baby to gladden their home.

Schubert's 'Notturno' *comes in under* Mary's *final speech. The lights fade.*

CONVERSATIONS
ON A
HOMECOMING

CONVERSATIONS

Conversations on a Homecoming was first performed by the Druid Theatre Company, Galway, on 16 April 1985 with the following cast:

TOM	Sean McGinley
MICHAEL	Paul Brennan
JUNIOR	Maeliosa Stafford
LIAM	Ray McBride
PEGGY	Marie Mullen
MISSUS	Pat Leavy
ANNE	Jane Brennan

Directed by   Garry Hynes
Designed by   Frank Conway
Lighting by   Barbara Bradshaw

Time and place: The early 1970s. A pub in a town in east Galway.

A run-down pub. Outside, perhaps on a glass panel above the door, the faded signboard reads THE WHITE HOUSE. *The place is in need of decoration, the stock on the shelves is sparse, a clock on a wall permanently reading ten past four, a dusty picture of John F. Kennedy . . . The only thing that appears to be new is a cheap partition which has been erected to divide the room into two, a Public Bar (not seen) and the Lounge which is the main acting area.*

The lights come up on ANNE. *She is seventeen, standing behind the counter, motionless, staring blankly out the window, her expression simple and grave. A tapping on the counter in the public bar; it is repeated before she reacts and moves off to serve a customer.*

TOM *is hunched in his overcoat, seated at a table, sipping from a half-pint glass of Guinness, reading a newspaper: his feet resting on the rung of another chair give him a posture that is almost foetal. He is in his late thirties.*

JUNIOR *is entering front door and hallway. He pauses in door to investigate momentarily the sound of a car pulling into the car park.* JUNIOR *is thirty-one, more casually dressed than the others (a duffel coat and a good heavy pullover), a contented, unaffected man; a big – though simple – sense of humour; an enviable capacity to enjoy himself. En route to the counter:*

JUNIOR: Well, bolix!

TOM (*mildly*): Oh? (*And continues with his newspaper.*)

JUNIOR (*at the counter, poking his head around the end of the partition*): Well, Anne! How yeh, Johnny! (*Exaggerated nasal brogue.*) We'll have fhrost!

Chuckle, off, in reaction: We will, a dhiabhail . . .

JUNIOR (*to* TOM): He didn't come in yet?

TOM: Was that him?

JUNIOR: No. What are you having, boy?

TOM: Pint.

JUNIOR: Two pints, Anne. (*To* TOM:) Liam Brady pulling into the car park. Well, Anne! Are you well?

ANNE (*almost silently; smiles*): Fine.

LIAM *entering, car keys swinging, about the same age as* JUNIOR; *well-dressed and groomed: expensive, heavy pinstripe, double-breasted suit, a newspaper neatly folded sticking out of his pocket for effect. He is a farmer, an estate agent, a travel agent, he owns property . . . he affects a slight American accent; a bit stupid and insensitive – seemingly the requisites of success.*

LIAM: Hi! (TOM *merely glances up.*) Hi, Junie!

JUNIOR: How yeh.

LIAM: What's bringing ye in here?

JUNIOR: Michael Ridge is home from America.

LIAM: Hi, Anne! (*Craning over the bar to see if there is anyone in the public bar.*)

JUNIOR: We'll get all the news. What are you having?

LIAM (*indecisive*): Ahm . . .

JUNIOR: It's all the same to me.

LIAM: Had me a few shots earlier. Pint.

JUNIOR: Three pints, Anne.

LIAM *joins* TOM, *takes out his newspaper, is not interested in it, is replacing/arranging it in his pocket again.*

TOM: Give us a look at that. What time is it?

LIAM: It's nearly eight.

TOM (*disinterestedly*): And what has *you* in here?

LIAM: Oh.

JUNIOR: Thanks, Anne. (*Takes first pint to table.*) There's only Johnny Quinn in the public bar.

Off, the town clock chiming eight.

LIAM: That town clock is fast.

JUNIOR: He was taking his mother or something out the country to see relations. I lent him the car.

TOM: I thought he said he might be here sooner.

JUNIOR: No. He said he'd hardly make it before eight. A reunion, wuw! We'll get all the news.

LIAM: He didn't bring a bus home with him then?

JUNIOR: No – Thanks, Anne – I lent him the car. (*Taking the other two pints to the table quietly.*) He was anxious to see JJ too.

LIAM: JJ was up in Daly's earlier. On another batter. Getting mighty opstreperous, fellas, mighty maudlin.

TOM (*to himself*): Are they singing up in Daly's? The cowboys.

JUNIOR (*suddenly*): I'm not staying out late tonight.

TOM: What? (*Chucks Liam's paper aside.*) And who's asking yeh?

They have been waiting for their pints to 'settle'. Off, the church clock is chiming eight.

LIAM (*a major triumph for his watch*): There, the church clock, eight!

TOM: Another discrepancy between Church and State.

LIAM: What?

TOM: Nothing. Good luck!

JUNIOR: Luck, boy!

LIAM: Good luck, fellas!

JUNIOR (*appreciative gasp after a long draught*): Aaa, Jasus! (*And starts to sing absently to himself:*) 'They were only a bunch of violets, violets so blue/ Fresh and fair and dainty, they sparkled like the dew/Fresh and fair and dainty, they sparkled like the dew/ But I'll not forget old Ireland far from the old folks at home.'

During this, MISSUS has come down the stairs (which are at the end of the hall), gone into the public bar – a greeting, off, to Johnny – and now reappears behind the counter in the lounge. She is in her early fifties, carelessly dressed (a dirty house-coat); a worried, slow-moving drudge of a woman, senses a bit numbed by life, but trying to keep the place together.

MISSUS: Aa, the boys.

JUNIOR: Hello, Missus! (*And continues another jumbled verse of the song to himself.*)

MISSUS: Yas.

LIAM: How do, Mrs Kilkelly!

MISSUS: And Liam.

She whispers something to ANNE and ANNE goes about collecting her coat to go on some errand.

LIAM: The partition is holding up well?

MISSUS: Yas. Thanks. Yas, Liam. (*Smiles/drools at LIAM, and she exits to public bar.*) Cold enough, Johnny?

JUNIOR (*to himself*): We'll have fhrost.

TOM: Shh!

TOM has been listening to a car pulling into the car park. ANNE is pulling on her overcoat going out front door when she bumps into MICHAEL who is entering.

MICHAEL: Oops!

ANNE: Sorry.

MICHAEL: Sorry.

A backward glance from ANNE at him as she exits. MICHAEL pauses for a brief moment to muster himself before going into the lounge. He is the same age as TOM; defensively inclined towards the supercilious, false panache to hide his failure.

MICHAEL: Hello there! –

JUNIOR: Hah, here he is! –

TOM: Oh, look in! –

LIAM: The man himself! –

MICHAEL: Gee! Gee! Lot of changes round here! –

TOM: Don't start that game now – How yeh, you're welcome, how yeh! –

LIAM (*pushing awkwardly through them, nearly spilling JUNIOR's pint*): Well, howdy, Mick! –

JUNIOR (*protecting his pint*): Jasus, the cowboy! (*Liam*) –

MICHAEL: Liam! And how are you? –

LIAM: Good to see yeh, well good to see yeh! –

TOM: That's a fancy-lookin' suit you have on. –

MICHAEL: What's fancy about it? –

TOM: Nothing. –

LIAM: You look just great! –

TOM (*shaking hands*): Well? How yeh, you're welcome, how yeh?

MICHAEL: Not too bad.

JUNIOR: Not three bad, what're you having, boy?

TOM: Oh, a brandy, a brandy, a brandy for the emigrant, don't yeh know well? –

LIAM: Pull up a pew, fella –

MICHAEL: I'll have a pint, Junie.

JUNIOR: Fair play to yeh. (*Going to counter.*) Missus!

TOM: Well!

MICHAEL: How are you?

TOM: I'm alright.

JUNIOR (*impatient at counter*): Missus!

TOM: You're lookin' well.

MICHAEL: Can't help it. You know?

TOM: I suppose you can't.

JUNIOR (*to* MISSUS *who has entered behind counter*): A pint, please.

LIAM: A holiday, Mick?

MICHAEL: Ah . . . yeh.

LIAM *nods in that solemn provincial way, eyes fixed on* MICHAEL *in ignorant assessment.*

And how are things with you, Liam?

LIAM: Fightin' fit, fella

MICHAEL: The farming, the rates collecting, the –

TOM: Oh and sure he's an auctioneer too now.

MICHAEL: Yeh?

LIAM: Estate agent, Mick.

TOM: Took out his diploma after intensive and in-depth study last year.

JUNIOR (*from counter*): MI5 AA!

MICHAEL: What?

TOM: Junior's sense of humour.

LIAM: MIAA, Mick.

JUNIOR: Letters after his name and the car he drives doesn't need a clutch!

MICHAEL: So business is good then?

LIAM: Property-wise, this country,

A-one, Mick. This country, Mick, last refuge in Europe.

MICHAEL: Good begod, I came to the right place then.

JUNIOR: Thanks, Missus. (*He is waiting for his change.*)

TOM: You haven't much of an accent.

MICHAEL (*British accent*): Only for the stage.

TOM (*British accent*): Yes, yes, good show, jolly good, right chaps, it's up to us, we're going through: John Mills.

MICHAEL: Aw, he's making better ones now.

TOM: Is he?

JUNIOR: Thanks, Missus.

MISSUS (*retreating off, fingering her dirty house-coat*): Aa, Michael.

We see her a few moments later reappear from the public bar into the hallway and going upstairs.

MICHAEL: How's your mother, Tom?

TOM: Oh, she's fine.

MICHAEL: And the school?

TOM: Fine. The headmaster might drop dead any day now –

JUNIOR (*setting pint in front of* MICHAEL): Now, boy –

TOM: And my subsequent rise in station and salary will make all the difference.

MICHAEL: Thanks, Junie.

TOM: What brought you back?

MICHAEL (*evasive*): Oh, before I forget them – (*He gives car keys to* JUNIOR.) Thanks.

JUNIOR: Not at all, boy.

TOM: Hmm? At this time of the year.

JUNIOR: Jasus, you weren't home for . . .

TOM: Must be ten years.

JUNIOR: That race week. (*He starts to laugh.*)

TOM: Aw Jay, that Galway race week!

They start to laugh.

JUNIOR: Aw Jasus, d'yeh remember your man?

TOM: Aw God, yes, your man!

JUNIOR: Aw Jasus, Jasus! (JUNIOR's laugh usually incorporates 'Jasus'.)

TOM: The cut of him!

JUNIOR: Aw Jasus, Jasus!

LIAM: Who?

JUNIOR: D'yeh remember?

MICHAEL: I do.

JUNIOR: But do yeh? – Jasus, Jasus!

LIAM: Who was this?

JUNIOR: Do yeh, do yeh, remember him?

MICHAEL (laughing): I do, I do!

JUNIOR: Jasus, Jasus!

JUNIOR's laugh is infectious, all laughing. Ritual toast again.

MICHAEL: Good luck, Junie!

JUNIOR: Good luck phatever (whatever)!

TOM: Good luck!

LIAM: Good luck, fellas!

They drink.

MICHAEL: Is JJ around?

TOM: No. But what brought you back?

MICHAEL glances at him, unsure.

So sudden. This time of the year.

JUNIOR: Nos-talgia.

MICHAEL: Something like that.

TOM: What?

MICHAEL (forces a laugh): The White House, our refuge, our wellsprings of hope and aspiration. (Mimicking JJ/ Kennedy:) Let the word go forth from this time and place to friend and foe alike that the torch has been passed to a new generation!

LIAM: JJ doing his Kennedy bit, is it? Making speeches. (Dismissive.) JJ.

MICHAEL (to LIAM): We virtually built this place with JJ. Right, Tom?

JUNIOR: Jasus we did.

MICHAEL: Night after night, while you were wasting all those years away at university.

JUNIOR: Jasus we did. And sank pints.

TOM (to JUNIOR): Sure you were only a boy.

MICHAEL: You wrote your rightest poems here.

TOM (laughing at himself): I did – and read them!

MICHAEL: You wrote that speech – JJ's inaugural – for our opening (JJ/ Kennedy voice again:) Friends, all this, our cultural centre has been a co-sponsorial job from design to décor. Mark its line, its adornment –

TOM: I never said 'mark' –

MICHAEL: Its atmosphere derives from no attribute of wild wisdom, vestige of native cunning, or selfish motive. The day of the dinosaur is gone forever. And with it the troglodytian attitude incarcerated in the cave whence it came

TOM: Troglodytical.

MICHAEL: And as I look around me, I know that some of us will be departing –

JUNIOR: To ride the waves or drown in them.

MICHAEL: That's it Junie –

JUNIOR (pleased with himself): As the fella says –

MICHAEL: To seek the new ideas. And some of us will remain, custodians of this, our White House, to keep the metaphorical doors of thought, hope, generosity, expression, aspiration open. So that all will find – the denizen of this hamlet, the traveller in his frequent returnings – a place of fulfilment, or a refuge if need be. Something like that. You wrote that.

TOM (chuckling): I suppose I did. Sure we'd all have been departing, riding the waves, if we paid heed to poor auld JJ.

LIAM laughs.

But you didn't tell us: What brought you back?

MICHAEL: I told you. Lost horizons.

TOM: Wha! (First wonderings: Can he be serious?)

MICHAEL: No.

TOM: What?

MICHAEL: No, you'd be surprised at how dicked-up one can get – I mean, how meaningless things can become for one – occasionally of course – away from one's – you know.

TOM: I suppose 'one' can. (*Awkward moment's pause.*) But you're looking well.

MICHAEL: Can't help it.

LIAM (*eyes all the time fastened on MICHAEL*): It could be a good stand for a fella, Mick? This place, properly handled.

MICHAEL (*joking*): You didn't consider taking up the gun and marching on the North?

JUNIOR: We thought about it.

MICHAEL *laughs.*

Serious.

MICHAEL: What?

JUNIOR: We did.

LIAM: We nearly did.

JUNIOR: Serious.

LIAM: Shoot us a few Prods.

MICHAEL *looks at* TOM.

TOM: It's very bad up there.

MICHAEL: I know, I've been reading, but.

LIAM: We nearly did, one night.

TOM: The way the Catholics are being treated.

MICHAEL (*trying to conceal his disbelief*): Yeh?

LIAM: A geezer up there in the papers one evening talking about coming down here and burning us all to the ground.

JUNIOR: We know where to lay our hands on a few guns.

LIAM: Well, I'm telling you, when I read that.

MICHAEL: Guns!

JUNIOR: We did. He (*TOM*) did.

MICHAEL (*laughs in disbelief*): You did, Tom?

TOM (*frowning*): What?

LIAM (*boasting*): I was awful drunk that night, I was awful sick – Did ye see me?

MICHAEL (*because* TOM *is still frowning*): No, I believe – I believe things are pretty bad alright, but, a baby and all now, Junie?

JUNIOR: Oh-oh.

MICHAEL: And how is Peggy, Tom?

TOM: Fine.

MICHAEL: Yeh? She's okay?

TOM: Fine. I sent her word we'd be in here.

MICHAEL: Any signs of ye doing it yet – as the saying goes?

TOM: Aren't we engaged, isn't that enough?

JUNIOR: Jasus, ten years engaged!

TOM (*mock belligerence*): Well, isn't it better than nothing!

JUNIOR (*laughing*): Aw Jasus, Jasus!

LIAM: But he's bought the site, Mick.

TOM: And isn't it doubled in value now!

LIAM: Trebled, trebled, fella!

JUNIOR: Jasus, ten years engaged!

TOM: D'yeh hear Sonny?

JUNIOR: Jasus, Jasus!

TOM: Napkin-head, procreation hope!

JUNIOR: What does that mean, sir?

TOM: Dick!

They laugh.
During this last, MISSUS *has come down the stairs, along hallway and is entering lounge, now minus her dirty house-coat, wearing her best cardigan.*

MISSUS: Aa, the boys. And Liam. You're welcome, Michael.

MICHAEL: Hello, Missus.

MISSUS: Welcome, yas, now.

MICHAEL: You're looking well.

MISSUS: Oh now, pulling the divil by the tail. Isn't that the way, boys? But your mother is delighted, yas, the surprise of your visit. I was talking to her for a minute this morning in the

post office and she was telling me.
Now.

MICHAEL: We were just saying we had some great times here, what?

MISSUS: Yas, but Liam is the boy that's doing well. Waiting for the right girl. And poor Tom waiting on you there this hour.

TOM: I am indeed, Missus, the hound.

MISSUS: Aa, sure he doesn't mean that at all. Usen't we call the two of you the twins one time. Always together, always together. D'ye know now. Yas.

JUNIOR (*quietly*): Yas, the twins.

MISSUS: Yas, the twins. Aa, I think Junior is a bit of a rogue.

TOM: A blackguard, Missus.

MISSUS: Aa, no joking. D'ye know now. A nice wife and a baby and a home of his own to go into. The way everyone should be.

JUNIOR (*to TOM*): Now.

MISSUS: Isn't that right, Liam?

LIAM: That is c'rrect, Mrs Kilkelly.

MISSUS: A nice sensible girl, and not be roaming the world.

JUNIOR (*to MICHAEL*): Now.

MICHAEL: How is JJ?

MISSUS: Oh JJ is – very well, thank you.

MICHAEL: The time of our lives putting this place together, we were just saying. Do you remember the night – Where's the painting of the nude?

MISSUS: Yas, but you're doing well, your mother was saying and are you alright there now, boys?

JUNIOR: Well, you might start filling another round. (*To* TOM:) Your round.

MISSUS: Certainly. (*Going back to the bar.*) Nice to see you all again.

JUNIOR: She's desperate slow on the aul' pints.

MICHAEL *is still looking after her, shaken by the transformation that has come over her.*

MICHAEL: She was the first lady. But

where is JJ?

TOM: Sure the man is dyin'.

MICHAEL: What!

TOM: Drinkin' himself to death, don't be talking.

LIAM: That's where she sent the young one, out looking for him.

MICHAEL: Did you tell him I'd be here? (JUNIOR *nods.*) And?

JUNIOR: He isn't together at all: he's on a batter.

MICHAEL: But you told him?

JUNIOR *nods.*

LIAM: He's probably gone into Galway or some place by now.

MICHAEL: But he'll show up?

TOM: You won't see him for a week. What about yourself?

LIAM (*pleasure of the anticipation on his face*): I'll have the selling of this place before long.

TOM: What about yourself?

MICHAEL: What?

LIAM: Gals.

JUNIOR: 'Gals'. Jasus, you have more of an American accent than him!

TOM: There was a rumour some time back you were married.

MICHAEL: No.

TOM: What?

MICHAEL: Free love.

TOM: Oh God!

MICHAEL: Who was the bird I bumped into at the door?

JUNIOR: Fair play to yeh!

MICHAEL: A young one.

LIAM: You never lost it, Mickeen!

MICHAEL: As a matter of fact I did. Plenty of it, too much of it over there.

TOM: What about our new bank clerk for him, June?

JUNIOR: Grrrrrah, Josephine!

TOM: We have a right one for yeh.

LIAM (*to himself*): Dirty aul' thing.

JUNIOR: She stays here and all: a quick nip up the stairs on your way out tonight and 'wham, bang, alikazam!'

TOM: The most ridiculous whore of all times.

JUNIOR: No bra.

LIAM: Dirty aul' thing.

MICHAEL: Why so ridiculous?

TOM: A bank clerk, a bank clerk! A girl in her position!

JUNIOR (*whispering*): And they say she wears no knickers either. Ich bin ein Berliner!

TOM (*frowning*): What were you going to say?

MICHAEL: No, but this young one at the door, that wasn't her.

LIAM: Who?

MICHAEL: A blue coat, fair, about eighteen.

JUNIOR: Anne. (*It doesn't register with* MICHAEL.)

TOM: Anne, Annette.

JUNIOR: Missus's daughter –

TOM: JJ's daughter.

MICHAEL (*brightening*): Well-well!

JUNIOR: She's turning out nice on me word?

MICHAEL: Annette. JJ's daughter. I bumped into her at the door and I got the whiff of soap, sort of schoolgirl kind of soap, and

TOM: It took you back?

MICHAEL: It did.

TOM: Tck!

MICHAEL: No, there's a distinctive kind of aroma off –

TOM: Gee, aroma. It'd be great to be young again.

MICHAEL: You're a bogman, Ryan.

TOM: I've no sensitivity alright.

They are chuckling. JUNIOR *draining his glass as* MISSUS *arrives with one pint which she puts before* LIAM.

MISSUS: Now, Liam. The other three are coming, boys. (*Returning to bar.*)

MICHAEL: Well, news!

Short pause; all thinking.

JUNIOR: Molloy's dog got killed by a tractor last month.

TOM: Did you hear Stephen Riley died?

MICHAEL: No!

TOM *nods.*

Hoppy?

TOM: Yeh, with the limp.

MICHAEL: Well did he?

TOM: He did.

JUNIOR: D'yeh remember the Christmas he split the wife with the crucifix? (*They laugh. Solemnly.*) The Lord have mercy on him.

He waits to meet their eyes and they burst into irreverent laughter.

TOM: And of course you know Larry, Larry O'Kelly got transferred?

MICHAEL: Yeh. I was looking around for his painting of the nude.

JUNIOR: Transferred, and *Bridget Reclining* with him.

MICHAEL: It used to hang there.

TOM: JJ defying Church and State hanging a nude.

JUNIOR: And the priest, Father Connolly – remember? – was up and down here, hotfoot about the nude.

TOM: That wasn't why –

JUNIOR (*taking fresh pint that was set before* LIAM): Here, cowboy, gimme that pint and I'll be working away on it.

MICHAEL: And JJ: 'I do not speak for the Church on public matters, Father, and the Church is not going to speak for me!'

JUNIOR: Good luck!

MICHAEL: And JJ sent Father Connolly packing.

TOM: He didn't.

MICHAEL: He did.

JUNIOR (*after appreciative draught*): Aaa, Jasus!

MICHAEL: 'When long-held power

leads men towards arrogance, art reminds them of their limitations!'

JUNIOR: Father Connolly called it a dirty picture.

TOM *and* MICHAEL *speaking simultaneously:*

TOM: He didn't!

MICHAEL: 'When long-held power narrows men's minds, art, poetry, music cleanses – '

TOM: He called it a *bad* picture –

MICHAEL: As far as you're concerned then, Father –

MICHAEL *and* JUNIOR *speaking simultaneously:*

JUNIOR: 'Art galleries – '

MICHAEL: 'Art galleries – '

MICHAEL *and* JUNIOR *laugh.*

MICHAEL: 'As far as you are concerned then, Father, art galleries all over the world are filled with dirty pictures?'

TOM (*playing Fr. Connolly*): Please, please – Boys! – please don't talk to me about art galleries. Holy Moses, I've visited hundreds of them. You see, boys, I am a man who has travelled the world – '

MICHAEL: 'I heard you spent a few years in Nigeria, but remember you're not talking to the Blacks now!'

JUNIOR *collects the other three pints, paying* MISSUS. MISSUS *and* JUNIOR *speaking simultaneously:*

MISSUS: Now, boys, yas.

JUNIOR: 'You're not talking to the Blacks now.'

TOM: Aw but do ye see? The arrogance and condescension which you impute to Fr. Connolly's remarks were only too evident in our swinging liberal JJ's statements.

MICHAEL: What does that mean?

JUNIOR: That's what I was going to say.

TOM *waives the question.*

LIAM: Good luck, fellas!

TOM: The reason, the *real* reason, behind Fr. Connolly's visits had nothing to do with the painting.

MICHAEL: He wanted JJ to take it down.

TOM: That was the *ostensible* reason. The real reason was to tell JJ to behave himself like a good boy, to *warn* him.

JUNIOR: And JJ *didn't* take it down – fair play to him.

MICHAEL: To *warn* him?

TOM: A token glance at the nude, a few token remarks about art galleries or something, and 'Haw-haw-haw, you are a son-of-a-bachelor, John-John.' The real reason. 'You see, John-John, pub, club, art-centre, whatever it is you are running here, people are growing concerned. And particularly since your trade to date seems to be in the young. Already there have been complaints, indeed visits to the presbytery from worried parents and other concerned parties.'

JUNIOR: The opposition, Paddy Joe Daly, and the other wise publicans.

TOM: 'One native son, a guileless youth it appears, is about to leave a respectable clerkship which I had a hand in getting him myself –'

MICHAEL: He never spoke for me!

TOM: 'And a widowed mother – '

MICHAEL: My mother never went near –

TOM: 'To go off to Dublin to become – of all things! – an actor.'

MICHAEL: Maybe your mother did.

TOM: 'While another is suddenly contemplating leaving a secure pensionable position. Think of it! A teacher! The first from the generations of plebs to which he belongs to make such breakthrough – to the professions! And going off without prospects, John-John, to God knows where!'

JUNIOR: To become a writer.

TOM: 'Others. Youths!'

JUNIOR: Taking to hard liquor – Wuw!

TOM: 'And all, it would appear, being influenced by something call the *vision* of a Johnny-come-lately.'

LIAM: That's right, fellas, JJ was a blow-in, a cute buff-sham from back there Caherlistrane-side.

TOM: 'Too far too fast for us, John-John.'

MICHAEL: And that was the warning?

TOM (*silent 'No'*): 'I think – John – you would be well advised to leave the decision-making to the parents and their spiritual advisors as to what is best for their children. I know you have it in you to take careful account of what I have said and the *security* of wiser steps.'

MICHAEL: That sounds more like a threat.

TOM: 'Holy Moses, Michael – John-John – we don't threaten anyone. We don't have to. We, the poor conservatives – troglodytes, if you will – have seen these little phases come and go. All we have to do is wait.'

MICHAEL *laughs. Then ritual toast:*

MICHAEL: Good luck!

TOM: 'God bless you.'

JUNIOR: Luck!

LIAM: Good luck, fellas!

MICHAEL: But he might show up.

TOM *shakes his head.*

Aw, you'd never know.

TOM *throws his head back at* MICHAEL'*s romantic hope springing eternal.*

LIAM: Strangers wanting to run the town.

MICHAEL: There was never anything like it before. And where did that lousy partition come out of?

TOM *and* JUNIOR – *with no great interest – notice the partition for the first time.*

LIAM: No decent heating in the place. The place was mighty cold without that.

MICHAEL: And how is Silver Strand?

LIAM: Oh! Oh!

JUNIOR: Tell him.

LIAM: Aw no, fellas!

JUNIOR: Tell him! The place is crawling

with priests and police since the bishop's niece got poled back there last year – Tell him.

LIAM: Well. Well, I shifted this Judy at a dance in Seapoint and wheeled her back to the Strand, and we were coorting away there nicely – No! No! A fair coort mind! I hadn't even bothered to let back the seats of the auld jalop. But next thing – suddenly – my heart was in my mouth. Tap-tap-tap at the window, and it all fogged up. A big policeman with a flashlamp. What are yeh doin' there, says he. Kneckin', fella, says I. Well, says he – Well, says he, stick your neck now back in your trousers and hump off.

They laugh.

JUNIOR: Tell him about Dooley.

TOM: Aw wait'll I tell yeh.

JUNIOR: Yeh remember Dooley?

MICHAEL: The librarian is it?

TOM: Shiny boots –

JUNIOR: Holy Harry –

TOM: First Mass, Communion, a pillar of the community. Well, it's all an act. He hates it all: Church, State, everything,

JUNIOR: Jasus, Jasus, Jasus . . .

TOM: Stall it a minute now. The headmaster sent me down to organise some kind of library service with him for the school and we got talking. And d'yeh know his great secret rebellion against it all? Called me down to the shelf like this. *The Life Story of the Little Flower* filed under horticulture. Well laugh when I saw it? I nearly died. And giggling away to himself. The malice! I never enjoyed anything so much. (*Laughter subsiding.*) Well yourself?

MICHAEL: Oh, having a great time. You know?

TOM: *News! News!*

MICHAEL: Well, I was with this buddy of mine one night and we picked up these two chicks in a bar.

LIAM: Yeh? –

JUNIOR: Yeh?

MICHAEL: Well. It was coming to

closing time anyway and they're clearing the glasses away, see, and one of the barmen – just like that – grabbed the glass out of one of the chick's hands –

LIAM: Yeh? –

JUNIOR: Yeh?

MICHAEL: And this buddy of mine – and he's only a little guy – took a swing at the barman, and the barman – and not at my buddy – but a swing at the chick. So I took a swing at the barman: Me! You know?

TOM: Missed.

MICHAEL: Yeh. And then, the most marvellous choreographed movement, three more barmen vaulting over the counter and –

TOM: You all ended up on your arses outside.

MICHAEL: Yeh. And then –

TOM: You all had to go back meekly for your overcoats . . . You told us ten years ago!

MICHAEL: . . . Well, I was at this party the other night and I don't know what came over me, but I did something crazy.

TOM: Yeh?

LIAM: Yeh? –

JUNIOR: Yeh? –

TOM: Yeh?

MICHAEL (evasive): . . . No, forget that. But, ah, forget that, I was in the Village – you know? – one of those Village bars there recently and –

TOM: No, the party the other night – you did something crazy – What were you going to say?

MICHAEL: Ah, that was nothing. But, one of those Village bars, and, and, listening to these two weirdos. One of them proving that Moses was in fact a stonecutter.

LIAM: Proving it?

MICHAEL: Proving it: dates, figures, blisters, the lot. And the other fella –

LIAM: The Ten Commandments!

MICHAEL: The other fella trying to get

in with his own thesis, 'Yeah, man, I dig, man, but do you believe Jesus Christ committed suicide?'

TOM: They're daft alright.

MICHAEL: It was very funny.

LIAM: And no one around to give one of them a box?

MICHAEL: It was very funny.

JUNIOR: Moses up the mountain chiselling away on the quiet behind a cloud.

MICHAEL: It was very funny, Junie.

JUNIOR: That's a good one.

But the general feeling is that it is not such a good one and there is a very brief pause.

LIAM: But you're faring out well over there, Mick?

MICHAEL: Yep.

LIAM: Hah?

MICHAEL: Oh, pretty good. I'm – I'm up for this part in a film, actually. And that tele a while back. And there's a possibility of a part in a stage play, but we don't know yet.

TOM: 'We'? Who?

MICHAEL: My agent.

TOM: Oh, *you* have an agent?

MICHAEL: I had an agent the last time I was home, what's wrong with an agent?

TOM: I didn't say there was anything.

MICHAEL: Everyone has an agent.

JUNIOR: Begobs I haven't.

MICHAEL: I'd say averaging ten – eleven grand over the past two/three years. That's not bad.

JUNIOR: Not bad he says and the few quid a week my auld fella gives me.

MICHAEL: What? Well, it's not bad. It's not good either. I know guys making fifty – a hundred grand a year.

JUNIOR: I know fellas making nothing.

TOM: So what? What are you telling us for?

MICHAEL: Well, I wouldn't have made it clerking around here.

TOM: You wouldn't.

JUNIOR: Or teaching.

TOM: What are you laughing at? – You wouldn't, you can say that again.

JUNIOR (*laughing*): You could sing that, sir!

TOM: Tck, Jack!

JUNIOR (*guffawing*): As the bishop said to the actress!

TOM: Shut up, you eejit!

JUNIOR (*continues laughing/singing*): 'Sure no letter I'll be wearin', for soon will I be sailing – ' (*To* MICHAEL:) Hey, did you bring any home with yeh?

Laughing subsiding.

MICHAEL: But I was in this place the other night.

TOM: The party, is it?

MICHAEL: No. Yes. But there was a guy there anyway –

TOM: Who?

MICHAEL: No, wait'll you hear this one, Tom. A fella, some nut, I didn't know him.

TOM: Yeh?

LIAM: Yeh? –

JUNIOR: Yeh? –

TOM: Yeh?

MICHAEL: Well, he went a bit berserk anyway.

JUNIOR: Beresk.

TOM: Shh!

MICHAEL: Well. He took off his clothes. (*He looks at them, unsure, his vulnerability showing; he is talking about himself.*) Well, he took off his clothes. Well, bollocks naked, jumping on tables and chairs, and then he started to shout 'No! No! This isn't it at all! This kind of – life – isn't it at all. Listen! Listen to me! Listen! I have something to tell you all!'

TOM: Making his protest.

MICHAEL: Yeh.

TOM: Yeh?

MICHAEL: Something to tell them all.

TOM: Yeh?

MICHAEL: Whatever – message – he had, for the world. But the words wouldn't come for him anyway. And. (*Moment's pause; then, simply:*) Well. Then he tried to set himself on fire. (*He averts his eyes.*)

LIAM: Women there, Mick?

MICHAEL: Yeh. (*Mustering himself again.*) Ah, it wasn't anything serious – I mean, a party, a weirdo job. They were only laughing at him.

TOM: Yeh?

MICHAEL: Well, that's it. (*Forces a laugh.*) They calmed him down – put out the flames, what?

TOM: Yeh?

LIAM: Yeh?

MICHAEL: Oh yes. (*Trying to laugh.*) but then, then, one of the women took off *her* clothes and started cheering 'Up the Irish, up the IRA!'

TOM (*quietly*): His protest really foiled.

MICHAEL: Yeh.

LIAM: He was *Irish*?

MICHAEL: What?

JUNIOR: But what was up with him?

LIAM: He was Irish?

MICHAEL: Ah . . . yeh.

JUNIOR: But what was up with him?

MICHAEL: I don't know. Maybe someone put something in his drink or – There were all sorts of things going round – I mean, we, *we* were only laughing at him.

LIAM: Did you know him, Mick?

MICHAEL: I mean, I was drunk out of my skull myself.

TOM: Yeh?

MICHAEL: Well, that's it. Then he started crying, put on his clothes, I suppose, and left. I thought it was a good one.

LIAM: Did you know him, Mick?

TOM: Well that's a good one. (*Exchanges glances with* JUNIOR.)

JUNIOR: 'Tis.

MICHAEL: I thought it was a good one.

LIAM: Did he pull the quare one?

MICHAEL: What?

LIAM: The one that took off her clothes.

MICHAEL (*extreme reaction*): Aw for Jesus' sake, Liam!

LIAM: I was only joking.

TOM: Well that's a good one.

JUNIOR: 'Tis.

MICHAEL (*he goes to the counter*): We need another round.

PEGGY *has entered the front door and hallway. Now poking her head in lounge doorway. She is forty.*

PEGGY: Hello, did he arrive, is he here, did he come? Ary how yeh, Ridge, y'auld eejit heh, you're as beautiful as ever, janeymack you're looking delicious, you're as welcome as the flowers in May!

MICHAEL: Peggy.

PEGGY: Look at you: gorgeous, and the suit!

MICHAEL: You're looking well.

PEGGY: Oh flattery, flattery! Holding my own –

MISSUS (*appearing for a moment to see who has arrived*): Aaa –

PEGGY: How long are you home for?

MICHAEL: Oh –

MISSUS: Peggy –

PEGGY: How long? Hello, Missus –

MICHAEL: Well –

PEGGY: A few weeks?

MICHAEL: Yeh. Well, we'll see.

PEGGY: Well you're a sight for sore eyes, you didn't change a bit, he's looking tip-top, isn't he?

TOM: Will you sit down –

PEGGY: Bejaneymack tonight, you're looking smashing.

TOM: Will you sit down and don't be making a show of yourself.

She sticks out her tongue at TOM, *pokes a finger in his ribs and sits on the arm of his chair, stroking his hair.*

TOM *making private world-weary faces to himself.*

PEGGY: When did you arrive?

MICHAEL: Last night.

PEGGY: Aa, did yeh?

MICHAEL: What are you having, Peggy?

PEGGY: Well, I'm going to have a gin and tonic in honour of yourself if his Nibs will allow me.

MICHAEL: Will we switch to shorts?

TOM: Oh? The Yank.

JUNIOR: The returned wank as the fella says.

MICHAEL (*calls*): The same again Missus, please!

TOM (*mocks belligerently – as is his style*): I'll have a whiskey.

JUNIOR: I'll stick to the pint.

LIAM: And a shot o' malt for me, Mike.

MICHAEL: Gin and tonic, Missus, three Scotch and a pint.

TOM: Irish!

MICHAEL: What?

TOM: Irish! Irish!

LIAM: And an Irish for me, Mike. Nothing but.

MICHAEL: One Scotch, Missus.

MISSUS: Thanks, thanks. Alright, Michael.

PEGGY: Well.

Short silence.

LIAM: 'Around the fire one winter's night the farmer's rosy children sat.'

TOM: Oh?

PEGGY: It's nice to see us all together again, isn't it, it's like old times.

TOM: Isn't there a chair over there for yeh!

JUNIOR (*vacating his chair*): Here, a girleen.

PEGGY (*tongue out at* TOM, *a finger in his ribs*): Sourpuss! (*And takes* JUNIOR's *chair.*)

JUNIOR (*belches*): Better out than your eye.

PEGGY: But tell us who you met over there, tell us all about the stars.

MICHAEL: Oh! (*Shrugs.*)

TOM *sighs.*

PEGGY: Did you meet what's-his-name?

TOM (*to himself*): Tck!

MICHAEL: You meet them all different times.

TOM (*to himself*): Do yeh?

MICHAEL: Peter O'Toole.

PEGGY: Aa go on.

JUNIOR (*impressed*): Did yeh, did yeh though?

LIAM: Old Lawrence himself.

MICHAEL: Jack Lemmon.

PEGGY: And the other fella, the long fella?

MICHAEL: No.

JUNIOR: Did you ever meet –

MICHAEL: Paul Newman, Al Pacino.

PEGGY: Louis Jordan?

MICHAEL: Who?

TOM: Hopalong Cassidy. (*To* JUNIOR:) Give us a cigarette.

JUNIOR: That big one, the Redgrave one – Veronica, is it?

TOM (*irritably*): Vanessa.

JUNIOR: Fine bird – Oosh! Big.

TOM: You must be a very popular fella over there, Michael.

JUNIOR: You must be a very familiar fella over there, sir.

TOM (*groans*): Isn't this awful.

JUNIOR: Jealousy will get you nowhere, Ryan.

TOM: D'yeh hear Jack, d'yeh hear Sonny, off-to-Palestine head. Palestine, was it, or the Congo, was it, Junie, you were going to a few years ago?

JUNIOR: You were the one always talking about travelling – JJ arranging things for you – you were the one was meant to be off doing the great things.

TOM: I never mentioned the Palestine Police Force.

JUNIOR (*laughing – as is the case with the others through the following*): I got married.

TOM: And look at the cut of you!

JUNIOR: Nice home, nice baba, nice wife, Gloria – (*Singing.*) Oosh, she has a lovely bottom – set of teeth.

TOM: Ah but sure, what harm, your children will travel, your son will.

JUNIOR: He won't be a schoolmaster anyway.

TOM: An architect in Canada.

PEGGY (*laughing shrilly*): Oh yes, he was telling us one night.

TOM (*philosophical sniff*): But d'yeh see what I mean, the way the people are here: passing the buck. Twenty-seven years of age –

JUNIOR: Thirty-one –

TOM: And he's talking about what a five-month old son is going to do.

JUNIOR: Trotsky!

TOM: Now! That's smiling Jack the Palestine Policeman!

JUNIOR: Now! The great writer: Did ye read his great socialist piece in *Boy's Own*?

TOM: Did you mend many carburettors today?

JUNIOR: Did yous give many slaps today?

He drains his glass: MISSUS *is approaching with a tray of drinks. She serves* LIAM *first as usual.*

MISSUS: Now, yas, that's the boy, Liam.

JUNIOR: Off to write his great book.

LIAM: Thank you, Mrs Kilkelly.

JUNIOR: But he had the first page wrote – the dedication, 'In gratitude to J.J. Kilkelly'.

TOM *reacts to this but bides his time.*

LIAM: A nation of drop-outs as that professor said on the Late Late Show.

MISSUS: When will we be seeing you on television, Michael, we do be watching?

MICHAEL: Well, it's a question of

whether the things I'm in are sold to here or –

But MISSUS *is already on her way back to the bar.*

MISSUS: Your pint is on the way, Junior.

JUNIOR: No hurry, Missus. (*Sighs, lamenting into his empty glass.*)

TOM: I never dedicated anything to anyone.

JUNIOR: You never wrote anything.

TOM: And I certainly never thought of dedicating anything to JJ.

JUNIOR: Off to travel round the world to gain experience, and look at him. lazier than Luke O'Brien's dog that has to lean up against the wall to bark.

Big laugh

PEGGY: Well, cheers, Michael!

MICHAEL: Good health, Peggy!

JUNIOR: Cathaoireacha! (*Chairs*)

PEGGY (*to* MICHAEL): You're a tonic.

LIAM: Good luck, fellas!

PEGGY: You're just what we needed.

JUNIOR (*again to his glass*): Yas.

PEGGY: But tell us all.

MICHAEL: Oh. You know?

PEGGY: Aa go on now, tell us all.

TOM *groans.*

What's up with you tonight?

TOM 'Tell us all.' What does that mean?

PEGGY *looks away, hurt.*

LIAM: The sooner you two mavericks get hitched, the better.

TOM: Did you hear the definition of the gentleman farmer? A fella who bulls his own cows.

LIAM (*through the laugher*): Ryan! . . . Ryan! One good heifer any day is worth two months of a teacher's salary pound for pound.

TOM: Sterling or avoirdupois, Liam?

Off, the town clock ringing nine. MISSUS *approaching with* JUNIOR's *pint.*

LIAM: Ryan! Ryan! I made four hundred and twenty-eight pounds on a single deal last week.

TOM: At a puffed up auction.

JUNIOR: God bless yeh, Missus.

LIAM: What?

TOM: Nothing. Good man.

MISSUS: Now.

MICHAEL *has risen to pay for the round but* LIAM *is now awkwardly on his feet, bumping into* JUNIOR, *in his haste.*

LIAM: No! No! It's my round! I'm getting this! –

JUNIOR (*protecting his pint*): Jasus! –

MICHAEL: This one is mine, Liam –

LIAM: No! No! Don't take anyone's money!

TOM: He's getting carried away.

LIAM: My round, fella! –

MISSUS: Sure it's alright, Liam. –

LIAM (*to* MICHAEL): I've a question for you in a minute.

MISSUS: Sure it's –

LIAM: No! And have one yourself, Mrs Kilkelly.

MISSUS: No thanks, Liam, you're too good. (*Returning to bar.*)

LIAM: As a matter of fact my salary last year was – Well, it was in excess – greatly in excess of any figure you mentioned, boy. How much tax did you pay last year?

TOM: Sit down! –

LIAM: How much? –

JUNIOR: Sit *down*! –

LIAM: For a little comparison, boy –

TOM: Sit down outa that! –

JUNIOR: For Jasus' sake! Good luck who stood!

MISSUS *returning with change for* LIAM.

MISSUS: Now, Liam. That's the man.

PEGGY: How's the lodger, Missus?

JUNIOR: Josephine, wuw!

MISSUS *laughs, catering for them.*

PEGGY (*aside to* MICHAEL): Were they telling you about the one?

MISSUS: Aa but she's nice.

JUNIOR: Very good-natured they say.

MISSUS: But talking to the lads and her tea waiting on here in there this two hours. (*Wandering out to front door.*) That's who I am waiting for now. (*Alone in front door.*) D'ye know now. (*Where she remains for some moments. And, off, the church clock is chiming nine.*)

PEGGY: The place is gone to hell, isn't it?

MICHAEL: I don't know. Not irreparably. But *who* put up that partition? This was all one room. Remember Tom, one of your socialist ideas to JJ. We were all very impressed: that there should be no public bar, no divisions or class distinctions.

LIAM: What d'yeh mean, not irreparably, fella?

MICHAEL (*not listening*): What? Get rid of that (*partition*) and see the space we'd have.

LIAM: I wouldn't like to be the fella to inherit the debts of this place.

MICHAEL: What are you on about all evening, Liam?

LIAM: You're not fond of America, Mick?

MICHAEL: This was our roots, Liam. This was to be our continuing cultural cradle: 'Let the word go forth from this time and place –' What? We could do it again! – Wake up, wake up, boys and girls! – 'with a constant flow of good ideas.'

TOM *laughs/snorts at* MICHAEL's *romanticism.*

What?

JUNIOR: We could!

TOM: Oh God, two of ye!

MICHAEL: But doesn't it seem a pity?

LIAM: That's okay, Mick –

MICHAEL: Well, doesn't it?

TOM: Create another pub?

MICHAEL: It was more than a pub.

TOM: Our culture, as indeed our nationalism, has always had the profoundest connections with the pub.

LIAM: That's okay, fella, I'm keeping my eye on it quietly. I've the customer already on my books that it suits.

PEGGY: Now. And poor Missus has other ideas. She thinks she has him earmarked for Anne.

LIAM (*cockily – and he is drunker than the others*): I'm in no hurry for any Anne, or any other Anne (*To* MICHAEL:) And, fella – fella! – that partition, out of the goodness of my pocket and my heart. Without obligation.

MICHAEL *looks at* TOM. TOM *has been waiting for him.*

TOM (*blandly*): Yeh?

LIAM: (*laughs*): Unless, of course, you or your agent or your dollars would like me to handle the purchase for you. (*Sings in celebration of himself.*) 'Put the blanket on the ground!' (*And drinks.*)

MICHAEL *looks at* TOM *again.*

TOM (*smiles blandly*): 'The torch has been passed to a new generation.'

JUNIOR (*has been puzzling over a song to himself*): 'The sheep with their little lambs, passed me by on the road' – How does that begin?

TOM (*still smiling blandly, cynically at* MICHAEL): Hmm?

JUNIOR: That was JJ's song.

MICHAEL: But. (*Drinks.*) No, but, Annette, come to think of it now, she looks like JJ.

PEGGY: Aa did you meet her? Isn't she a dote?

TOM: That's an extraordinary observation, Michael, seeing you didn't recognise her when you saw her.

MICHAEL: Aw, she does, does, looks like JJ.

PEGGY: But what has you home at this awful time of the year?

TOM: Hope, refuge, to drink from his wellsprings, the romantic in his fancy suit.

MICHAEL: It'd be no harm if you smartened yourself up a bit.

TOM (*going to counter*): You'll have to do better than that. Missus! Give us a packet of cigarettes. Ten Carrolls.

JUNIOR (*still trying to work it out*): 'The sheep with their little lambs passed me on the road.'

MICHAEL: What's your news, Peggy, they told me nothing.

PEGGY: Did they tell you we have a new priest?

MICHAEL: No. What's he like?

TOM: Ridiculous. Jesus, the last fella was bad, Fr. Connolly was a snob, but at least that's something: this fella is an eejit.

PEGGY: For as much as you see of the church to know what he is.

TOM: Ah, but I went to check him out. My dear brethern – This was his sermon one Sunday. (*A warning to* PEGGY:) Don't interrupt me now. A maan (*man*) wan time, wan place, somewhere, that kept leaving the church before the maas (*Mass*) was ended, and continued this maalpractice though repeatedly warned about it. An' wan Sunday, my dear brethern, wasnt he sloppin' outa the church wance again, an' just as he was steppin' outside didn't he look up at the clock to see what time 'twas, and d'yeh know what happend to him? – d'ye know what happened to him! The church clock fell off the tower on top of him. Now! Killed stone dead.

PEGGY: Oh that's exaggerated, love.

TOM: Ridiculous. In this day and age! And the young ones are worse, falling over backwards, arse over elbow, to talk about sex to show how progressive they are. Sex: progressive – Jesus! – Ridiculous – Smoke? (*To* JUNIOR.)

PEGGY: You never see any good in the Church.

TOM: Aa but I do, love. Look at Liam there, and he's a regular churchgoer. And think of how the marriage figures all over the country would have slumped again only for all the young nuns jumping over the wall and the young priests waiting for them outside with their cassocks lifted.

PEGGY: Oh that's not right.

TOM: Ridiculous. Tell us something, Ridge, anything, something interesting, for God's sake.

PEGGY: . . . You got quiet or something, Michael. Tell us how are all the girls treating you? Oh, there was a rumour some time back – Wasn't there, love? – that you were married.

MICHAEL: No.

PEGGY: What?

MICHAEL: I answered that one.

PEGGY: What?

MICHAEL: Well, there was a girl – some time back. I knew her quite well – intimately – know what I mean? She was working in this night club, and this guy starts chatting her up, charming her, et cetera.

LIAM: Yeh?

JUNIOR: Big bird?

MICHAEL: But this guy, he had a few bucks anyway, a yacht and all that, and he was trying to persuade her to go off on a trip with him.

JUNIOR: Yi-yi!

MICHAEL: That's the point. Eventually she did, the two of them alone on the boat for three weeks and he never tried to make her, never laid a hand on her. And she committed suicide.

TOM: Ary Ridge!

MICHAEL: I thought that would be your reaction.

LIAM: What?

TOM: Tck!

PEGGY (*smiling/frowning*): Did she drown herself or what Michael?

LIAM: A good boot in the arse she wanted.

MICHAEL: He was a sadist or something.

JUNIOR: He was a gomey if you ask me.

TOM: And what's to signify in that story?

MICHAEL: I knew her. She was – a friend. And I knew him.

TOM (*rising*): Ridiculous country. the luck is on me I never left here. (*Calls:*) You might as well start filing the acthoring man's round, Missus!

MICHAEL: Better make them doubles.

TOM: Oh?

MICHAEL: Some people need the stimulation.

TOM *laughs and exits to the Gents.*

PEGGY: But you must go into a lot of queer places over there?

MICHAEL: Maybe they'd only be 'queer' to people from round here.

MISSUS: Doubles, Michael?

MICHAEL: Yes! Why not!

PEGGY: Oh, did they tell you they nearly marched on the North one night?

MISSUS: And a pint for you, Junior?

JUNIOR: Aye-Aye, Missus.

PEGGY: Did they tell you?

LIAM: You're not a political animal, Mike?

MICHAEL: Excuse me, Liam, but no one round here ever called me Mick, Mike or Mickeen, okay?

LIAM *nods, gravely bovine.*
MICHAEL *offering cigarettes around.*
PEGGY *accepts one unconsciously.*
JUNIOR *singing snatches of 'All in the April Evening'.*

PEGGY: But you're getting on well over there?

MICHAEL: Strugglin'. Smoke, Junie?

PEGGY: Aa go on but are –

JUNIOR: Thanks boy –

PEGGY: But are yeh getting on well though?

MICHAEL: Yep.

LIAM: Never use 'em.

PEGGY: But seriously, are you? (*He is lighting her cigarette.*)

MICHAEL: Yes.

JUNIOR: 'The sheep with their little lambs . . .'

PEGGY: Oh I didn't want this at all. (*But she puffs away at it.*) But do yeh like it all the time?

MICHAEL (*irritably*): Yes, Peggy, it's marvellous.

PEGGY: I see.

MICHAEL: And how are things with you?

PEGGY: Oh now.

MICHAEL: What?

PEGGY: Oh indeed.

MICHAEL: Yes?

PEGGY: Oh now, don't ask me.

MICHAEL: You gave up the dressmaking, didn't you?

PEGGY: Well, yeh know, around here.

MICHAEL: And the singing?

PEGGY: What singing? (*Remembering, laughing shrilly.*) Oh yes! JJ and his classical music, and he having me up to the nuns taking singing lessons. Wasn't I the eejit? And wait'll I tell yeh, (*Whispering.*) I had a crush on him. That slob. And he old enough to be my father. I'm not saying anything, it was all in innocence. And Sister Jerome, the singing teacher, tone deaf.

JUNIOR: 'Passed me by on the road.'

MICHAEL: Who was the slob?

PEGGY: JJ! Wait'll Tom comes back. (*He'll tell you*)

MICHAEL: So, you're minding the house with your mother?

PEGGY: Oh but I do a morning or two a week, now and again, bookkeeping for the vet.

MICHAEL: And how is that old friend of yours, Helen Collins?

PEGGY: Isn't she married? Sure you must have known – She's producing like mad. Well, three and one on the way, as they say. But she's let herself go to hell – Hasn't she, Junie? – I'm meant to look like her daughter and she's ten months younger than me.

MICHAEL: I see.

PEGGY: But sure you must have known, wasn't she an old flame of yours? (*She pauses for only the briefest moment not wanting to acknowledge the thought that he has been getting at her.*) Oh but they're hopefully going to open a tourist office here next year – Isn't that right, Liam? – and I'm in the running for it (*A smile at* LIAM.) if I know the right people. (*Then smiling bravely, a glance at* MICHAEL, *then averts her eyes.* MICHAEL *feeling ashamed of himself, looks at her empty glass and his own.*)

MICHAEL: That's – That's great. Hang on.

He goes to the counter and returns with his own and PEGGY's *drink.*

LIAM: An' so was Beethoven, fellas. Stone deaf.

MICHAEL (*toasting* PEGGY): The best! Those curtains are yours.

PEGGY: And I was up all night finishing them. And never got paid.

MICHAEL: We didn't want to get paid.

PEGGY (*impulsively, she throws her arms around him*): Ary, yeh daft aul romantic, it's lovely to see yeh! Oh gosh-golly, this is gone out again.

MICHAEL *relights her cigarette.* MISSUS *approaching with* TOM's *and* LIAM's *drinks.*

MISSUS: I'll clear a few of these glasses out of yer way now.

JUNIOR: And the pint, Missus?

MISSUS: That's coming, Junior.

JUNIOR *sighs to himself.*

PEGGY: And d'yeh know? I could whistle the whole of the Sixth Symphony from beginning to end.

TOM (*returning from Gents*): They're daft alright.

PEGGY: Stop now, we were having a lovely time while you were out.

TOM: But do you yourself take questions like that seriously now?

PEGGY: Cheers, Michael!

MICHAEL: Cheers!

LIAM: Luck, fellas!

TOM: Michael?

MICHAEL: Questions like what?

LIAM: Questions like did Jesus Ch – Did you-know-who commit suicide.

TOM: And questions of the immoral and unethical behaviour of not screwing a bird on a boat.

MISSUS *returning to the bar.*

And, as Liam so delicately put it, for the proprietress's and my fiancée's sensitivities no doubt, questions like do you believe did you-know-who commit suicide.

MICHAEL: What's up with you?

TOM (*philosophical sniff*): Aw now.

JUNIOR (*to himself*); Aw fuck this! – Missus! – (*Striding to the bar, frustrated by his empty glass.*) Give me a drop of the hard tack too, and as well as the pint you're filling *now* you might start filling *another* pint for whoever is buying the next round.

MICHAEL: What's up with you?

TOM: Aw now.

PEGGY: You've changed, Michael.

MICHAEL: *I've* changed?

PEGGY: You used to be a grand shy lad with just the odd old, yeh know, flourish.

TOM: And supercilious with it.

MICHAEL: Well, I never nearly marched on the North, and I never thought a bank clerk is any more ridiculous for what she does than anybody else, and I never thought the jackboot in the arse was the cure for everything, and I never thought –

LIAM: Hold it, fella –

MICHAEL: That you (*Tom*) did either –

LIAM: Right there, fella –

MICHAEL: And to think of it! –

LIAM: Fella! –

MICHAEL: We were going to change all this!

LIAM: Fella!

TOM: You're missing the point –

MICHAEL: In this very room! And now it's bollocks talk about Protestants –

TOM: No one said anything about –

MICHAEL: The great anti-cleric (*Tom*) nearly going off to fight a Holy War!

TOM: No one said anything about –

LIAM: A minority Catholic group being oppressed! –

MICHAEL: You must be very unhappy in your lives –

TOM: Nothing to do with clerics –

LIAM: Fella! –

TOM: It's your ridiculous attitude –

LIAM: Brave Irish Catholic men and women –

MICHAEL: Everything seems ridiculous to you –

TOM: Women and sex orgies and some myth in your mind about JJ –

LIAM: Because – because a discriminating majority –

MICHAEL: You're really into 1917 –

TOM: What's all this about JJ? –

LIAM: A discriminating and – And! – gerrymandering majority! –

MICHAEL: Back to the stuck-in-the-mud-festering ignorance! –

TOM: 'Wellsprings and lost horizons'! –

MICHAEL: Yes! –

LIAM: A gerrymandering! –

MICHAEL: Lost horizons! –

LIAM: Fella, fella! A gerrymandering majority! –

TOM: Never arriving at reality –

LIAM: You can't deny it, you can't deny it – And! –

TOM: All mixed up –

LIAM: And! Racial memory, boy! –

TOM: Stop, Liam –

LIAM: Deny that one, boy! –

TOM: Stop, Liam! –

LIAM: Cause you can't deny it! – And! – And! – You can't deny it! –

TOM: Stop! –

LIAM: Cause – cause! – Fella! – Fella! –

TOM: Stop-stop-stop!

LIAM: You can't deny it!

TOM: Stop, will you, Liam! – Stop! – Forget that.

LIAM: I will not forget it! (*Forgetting it.*) I will not forget it.

TOM: You and your kind with your rose-coloured lights that you can switch on and off so easily. You don't want reality.

MICHAEL: Well, if yours is the reality.

TOM: Oh?

MICHAEL: Reality is always about poverty, is it?

TOM: No, it's always about flowers. Look, excuse me, Michael –

But LIAM *is off again.*

LIAM: And there's a thing called Truth, fella – you may not have heard of it. And Faith, fella. And Truth and Faith and Faith and Truth inex – inextricably – inextricably bound. And-And! – cultural heritage – you may not (have) heard of it – No border, boy! And cultural heritage inex-inextricably bound with our Faith and Hope and Hope and Faith and *Truth*! And some of us, and some of us, at least, cherish and – cherish and – and – are not supercilious, boy, with it – about it. Fella! I will not forget it! Last refuge in Europe.

TOM: Fine, Liam. Rest yourself now.

JUNIOR (*in answer to a glance from* LIAM): Well spoken, boy.

TOM: Look, excuse me, Michael, but what is the point, the real issue of what we are discussing!

MICHAEL: Well, maybe I have changed, because my enjoyment in life comes from other things than recognising my own petty malice in others.

TOM: Is that the point?

MICHAEL: A simple matter – and it's not a dream – of getting together and doing what we did before.

TOM: Is that the point? To do what we did before? And tell me, what did we do before?

MICHAEL: To do what we did before.

TOM (*to himself*): Jesus! Extraordinary how the daft romantics look back at things.

MICHAEL: Why is everyone calling me a romantic?

TOM: It's more polite.

MICHAEL: You would never have made the statements you are making tonight a few years ago.

LIAM: I'd reckon, fella, that proves he ain't static.

MICHAEL: It depends on which direction he went.

LIAM: I'd reckon, fella, that you are all – (*washed-up*)

TOM: No. Hold on. I think you're serious, Michael, hmm? I think he's serious. I think we have *another* leader. Another true progressive on our hands at last, lads. Another white fuckin' liberal.

PEGGY: Shh, love.

TOM: Home to re-inspire us, take a look at our problems, shake us out of our lethargy, stop us vegetating, show us where we went wrong –

MICHAEL: You're choosing the words –

TOM: Show us that we're not forgotten, bringing his new suicidal fuckin' Christ with him.

PEGGY: Love –

MICHAEL: Vegetating, lathargy, forgotten –

TOM: And most surprisingly, I think the poor hoor – like his illustrious predecessor – does not know where he is himself.

MICHAEL (*laughs*): I've been having a great time –

TOM: No – No! –

MICHAEL: Marvellous time!

TOM: You're too depressed, Jack, too much on the defensive Jack –

MICHAEL: Marvellous! But cheers anyway, Jack, cheers!

TOM: The point, Michael, the real point and issue for you, Michael – D'yeh

want to hear? You came home to stay, to *die*, Michael.

LIAM: Correct.

TOM: And fair enough, do that, but be warned, we don't want another JJ.

MICHAEL (*laugh/smile is gone*): I never mentioned I had any intention of staying home.

LIAM: Correct.

MICHAEL: What do you know about JJ?

LIAM: Enough, fella. But leave it to me, I'll rescue this place shortly.

MICHAEL: You spent so much of your time away as a student, the story was they were going to build a house for you in the university.

TOM: Michael.

MICHAEL: And you know nothing about JJ either.

TOM: I'm marking your card for you. JJ is a slob.

MICHAEL: He –

TOM: A slob –

MICHAEL: Wasn't –

TOM: Is, was, always will be. A slob. He's probably crying and slobbering on somebody's shoulder now this minute, somewhere around Galway. Missus in there treats him as if he were a child.

JUNIOR (*angrily, rising*): And what else can the woman do?

TOM: I'm just telling him.

JUNIOR (*exits to Gents*): Jesus!

MICHAEL: Why?

TOM: Why what?

MICHAEL: Why are you telling me – and glorying in it?

TOM: JJ is a *dangerous* and weak slob. He limped back from England, about 1960. England was finished for him. He could not face it again. I hope this is not ringing too many bells for you personally. And he would have died from drink, or *other* things, but for the fact that the John F. Kennedy show had started on the road round about then, and some auld women in the town pointed out doesn't he look like John F. Kennedy. And JJ hopped up on that American-wrapped bandwagon of so-called idealism –

MICHAEL: He had his own idealism.

TOM: Until he began to think he *was* John F. Kennedy.

MICHAEL: And, in a way, he was.

TOM: And Danny O'Toole up the road thinks he's Robert Mitchum and he only five feet two?

MICHAEL: He re-energised this whole town.

TOM: And Danny O'Toole is winning the west for us? Then people started to look at our new slob-hero afresh. People like Missus in there – she pinned her hopes on him – and, he quickly hopped up on her too. And so became the possessor of her premises, which we, and others put together for him, restyled at his dictates into a Camelot, i.e., a thriving business for selling pints.

MICHAEL: No –

TOM: Alright, selling pints was a secondary consideration. Like all camelot-pub owners he would have welcomed a clientele of teetotallers. His real purpose of course was to foster the arts, to give new life to broken dreams and the – procreative? – horn of immortality, nightly, to mortal men . . . But then came the fall.

MICHAEL: The assassination.

TOM: Of whom?

MICHAEL: Kennedy.

TOM: Oh, I thought for a minute there you were talking about *our* president, JJ.

MICHAEL: Well.

TOM: What?

MICHAEL: Well, as I heard it, after Kennedy's death, the *character*-assassination of JJ started in earnest.

TOM: No.

MICHAEL: Well, as you said yourself earlier, the priest's visits, other people's visits and the people the priest represented.

TOM: No. After Kennedy's assassination, the grief, yes. We all experienced it. But is grief a life-long profession?

MICHAEL: A lot of people feared and hated JJ in this town.

TOM: Feared? No. Never.

MICHAEL: Well, even on the evidence of tonight one could easily get the impression that this town could have had a few things – just a few, Tom? – to do with 'our' president's fall.

TOM: No! Look, he hopped up on the load of American straw and he had so little going for him that when that load of straw went up in smoke, JJ went up with it. Oh yes, they hated him – Why wouldn't they: Puppetry, mimicry, rhetoric! What had he to offer anyone? Where were the facts, the definitions?

MICHAEL: Why are you getting so excited?

TOM: I'm not getting excited. He-fed-people's-fantasies. That all he did. Fed – people's – fantasies.

MICHAEL: People are afraid of realising themselves.

TOM: Look, look, look – lookit! – (*to himself:*) Shit!

MICHAEL: They fear that.

TOM: Realising themselves? Like you did? Look! – Lookit! – leaving aside the superficial fact that he looked like John F. Kennedy – somewhere around the left ball – he could just as easily have though he was John McCormack or Pope John. He had so little going for him and we are such a ridiculous race that even our choice of assumed images is quite arbitrary.

MICHAEL: Are you finished?

TOM: The only mercy in the whole business, as I see it, is that he did not in fact think he was John McCormack.

LIAM: Man, Tomeen!

MICHAEL: JJ's respect, opinion and esteem for you –

TOM: To thine own self be true? God we're a glorious people alright.

LIAM: C'rrect.

LIAM *has risen and is going to Gents.*

TOM: Look, don't fret yourself about not seeing him tonight –

MICHAEL: I haven't given up on seeing him tonight.

TOM (*groans*): Aw Lord. There are plenty of JJs about. (*Pointing at* LIAM *who is exiting to Gents:*) I prefer that.

MICHAEL: You won't listen to my interpretation?

PEGGY: Aa, lads –

TOM: By all means – if you have one.

MICHAEL: JJ's opinion of you –

TOM: And if it's a sensible one.

MICHAEL: The *esteem* he held you in, always, way above the rest of us –

TOM: Ah-ah-ah-ah! Don't try that one. Remember where you are now. It's clear from the way you've been talking all night that the – innocence – naiveté of New York has softened your head, but remember you're talking to the people of a little town in the west of Ireland now: a little more sophisticated than that for us, Michael

MICHAEL: JJ and his wife, his first wife, were walking along a street, and –

TOM: In England?

MICHAEL: Yes.

PEGGY: Lads.

TOM: Just making sure I'm following facts.

MICHAEL: And a car came along, the steering was perfect, the driver was sober, but the driver was some poor unhappy bitter little prick who wanted to kill someone, anyone, and he drove the car up on the footpath and knocked JJ's wife over, and she died in hospital three months later.

TOM: Yes.

MICHAEL: And that's what you describe as the 'limp' JJ came into this town with?

TOM: Yes?

MICHAEL: What do you mean 'yes'?

TOM: Yes. I heard that story, and I'm sorry for him – if it's true.

MICHAEL: What?

TOM: No-no-no. Like, there are a lot of things we heard and believed some years ago, but we're a little older now.

MICHAEL: A man – after a tragedy like that –

TOM: More interesting stories are emerging now about JJ's past.

MICHAEL: To pull himself together after a tragedy like that and start afresh.

TOM: Look, I don't recall anybody ever reading any headlines about that tragic and dramatic event.

PEGGY: He made it up, Michael.

TOM (*to* PEGGY): Keep out of it. And people are now of the opinion that JJ was never married before, that there was no first wife, that there was only a bird, and there was no –

MICHAEL: Jesus, you're exceeding yourself! What's happened to you?

TOM: Alright, there *was* an accident! – and you can drag your own limp into it and your own grandmother as well – but it does not change the fact of the point we are *now* discussing, which is that JJ is, was, always will be a slob. Now, can you contradict me?

MICHAEL: I like him.

TOM: A-a-a-w! Back to the flowers. How nice, how fey, how easy for you. 'I like him.' And the way he upset and thwarted and wilfully and irresponsibly inflated and abused people. When I think of it. 'Together let us explore the stars.' Jesus!

JUNIOR *comes out of the Gents: his hand up for attention: he had got the first line of the song.*

JUNIOR: I've got it! 'All in the April evening'.

TOM (*to himself*): And left them high and dry.

PEGGY (*catering for him*): And bills outstanding all over the country, love, didn't he?

An angry grimace/gesture from TOM:
*he does not want her comments. Junior
– this is not his game – goes to the bar
and stays there for some moments.*

JUNIOR: Missus! Throw us out that
other pint.

TOM: God, we're a glorious people
alright. Half of us, gullible eejits,
people like yourself, ready to believe in
anything. And the other half of us –

MICHAEL: People like yourself, ready
to believe nothing.

TOM: People like yourself – people like
yourself – ready to believe, get excited,
follow to the death any old bollocks
with a borrowed image, any old JJ who
has read a book on American politics
or business methods. Jesus, images:
fuckin' neon shadows.

PEGGY: Love.

TOM: And the other half of us ready to
believe in nothing.

TOM: No! You don't understand! Never
the sound, decent, honest-to-God man
for us. Never again in this world, for
us, or for anyone else.

JUNIOR *joins them.*

JUNIOR: Good luck, fellas.

Silence.

MICHAEL (*quietly*): He nearly made it.

TOM: 'Nearly'? I thought you were
knocking us for that world a few
minutes ago?

MICHAEL: He was great.

TOM: In what way? When? – How? –
Where – Convince me! – Tell me!

MICHAEL: He hadn't got over the first
knock when the second happened.

TOM: Isn't that my proof, isn't that the
test of a man? Sure all you're
mentioning is his – dubious –
misfortunes and some kind of
hypothetical potential. What did he
achieve? What was he talking about?

MICHAEL: I don't know what he was
talking about, but wasn't he right?

TOM: Tck! . . . That's fine, you don't
know, that concludes the matter.

MICHAEL: Did you believe too much in
him?

TOM: Now, I like that. You're coming
up to our standards after all.

MICHAEL: Do you feel he let you down
personally or what?

TOM: The gentle romantic has his subtly
nasty side.

MICHAEL: Did you hope too much in
him? – Was he your only lifeline?

TOM: No, I didn't hope too much in
him, and I never ran messages for him
or fell flat on my face for him.

MICHAEL: He didn't ask you to –

TOM: Bloody sure he didn't.

MICHAEL: Because you were the –
doyen? – of his group.

TOM: I wouldn't have minded him
succeeding – but I had him taped from
the start.

JUNIOR (*a warning that* MISSUS *has
appeared*): Yas, enough dialectics as
the fella said.

But MISSUS *has come outside the bar-
counter to intercept* LIAM *who is
entering from the Gents and slip him a
drink on the house and have a fawning
word with him.*

TOM: I can see you're not the wide-eyed
boy who left here –

MICHAEL: Thanks –

TOM: But since you have nothing to
offer but a few distorted memories,
and a few personal tricks on the
burning monk caper, I'm marking your
card. You've come home to stay, die,
whatever – and you're welcome – but
save us the bullshit. We've had that
from your predecessor. We won't put
up with it again. Don't try to emulate
him, no re-energising, cultural cradles
or stirring that old pot. Now I know
you have it in you to take careful
account of what I've said, and the
security – Michael! – of wiser steps.

MICHAEL: Are you threatening me?

TOM: Holy Moses, Michael! – Me twin!
– We don't threaten anyone. We don't
have to! All we have to do – all we
have ever had to do – is wait! (*He
laughs.*) We leave it at that? God bless
you.

MICHAEL: I'm not sure what I came

home for, but I think I'm finding out.

LIAM *and* MISSUS *joining them.*

LIAM: Leave that matter to me, Mrs. Kilkelly.

MISSUS: Better looking this man (LIAM) is getting every day, isn't he? D'ye know now. Yas. You didn't bring a blondie home with you, Michael?

MICHAEL: There are dark-haired girls in America too, missus.

MISSUS: Musha, God help them. Be careful of them American ladies, a mac (*son*).

MICHAEL (*pointedly looking about*): How's business, Missus?

MISSUS: Oh, well, now, the off-season. Isn't that it, Liam?

LIAM: That is c'rrect, Mrs Kilkelly.

MISSUS: And things'll be picking up for us soon. Now.

MICHAEL: What you should do is get in a few of the natives telling funny stories for the tourists, and singing. And when things get going you could move out with the family and live in the henhouse for the season.

MISSUS: Isn't that what they're doing, some of them, living with the hens, to make room for tourists. And some of them, Michael –

MICHAEL: Yes. I didn't pay you for the last round.

MICHAEL *is standing, a roll of money ostentatiously in his hand.* MISSUS *feels offended by his cutting her short.*

MISSUS: Five pounds and sixty-nine new pence. Yas, your mother is delighted: I was talking to her for a minute this morning in the post office and she drawing out a wad of money. (*All get the implications of her remark. She gives* MICHAEL *change out of her cardigan pocket.*) Thanks, Michael. That's the woman with the money.

JUNIOR: Looking for a girl he is, Missus, wasn't he admiring the daughter?

MISSUS: Aa, Annette.

PEGGY: Aa, she's a dote. What's she going to do, Missus?

JUNIOR: I bet she wants to be an air hostess.

MISSUS: The cute Junior: how did you know that now?

JUNIOR: Oh-oh!

MISSUS: No. We were thinking of the bank. (*A glance at* LIAM.) Well, for the meanwhile, that is.

JUNIOR: Speak of an angel!

PEGGY: Oh hello, Anne.

ANNE (*silently*): Hello.

ANNE *has come in. She moves aside with* MISSUS *to report briefly in a whisper – little more than a shake of her head. (She has not found her father)* MISSUS *contains a sigh.*

PEGGY: The lovely coat.

MISSUS: And any sign of Josephine?

ANNE: She's up in Daly's lounge. She said she had a sandwich and not to bother with her tea.

MISSUS: Alright.

MISSUS *wanders off, out to the front door, sighs out at the night, then exits upstairs. And, meanwhile,* ANNE *is taking off her coat and moving to attend the bar.*

TOM: Anne! Come 'ere a minute. D'yeh know our acthoring man, Michael Ridge?

MICHAEL: D'yeh not remember me?

She has a natural shyness but it does not efface an interest she has in him.

Hmm?

ANNE: I do.

MICHAEL: What?

ANNE: I remember you here with Daddy.

MICHAEL: How is he?

ANNE: Not so good. (*She looks up at him, gravely, simply, for his reaction. He nods, simply, his understanding. Then she smiles.*) You're welcome home. (*And they shake hands.*)

TOM (*without malice*): Gee, kid, you were only so high when I saw you last.

MICHAEL: Is it Anne or Annette?

She shrugs: her gesture meaning that the choice is his.

Anne.

She nods, smiles, a silent 'okay'.

You're finished school?

ANNE: Three months time.

MICHAEL: And you won't be sorry.

ANNE: No. (*And she laughs.*)

PEGGY: Dreadful people, the nuns. Dreadful. Sister Bartholomew is the worst, don't you think, Anne?

ANNE: Isn't she dead?

PEGGY (*laughing shrilly*): Oh God yes, I forgot! I'm awful. But they're dreadful tyrants.

ANNE *is already moving away.*

MICHAEL: Will you come back and join us?

ANNE (*a toss of her head, smiling back at him*): I might.

TOM: Is it Anne or Annette, Michael?

MICHAEL: And she *is* like JJ. Well, things are looking up!

JUNIOR: Will we go up and have a few in Paddy Joe Daly's?

MICHAEL: The opposition, the enemy? No! We're grand here now.

JUNIOR: We'll introduce you to Josephine –

TOM   ⎫ Grrrah!
JUNIOR ⎭ Grrrah!

PEGGY: but were they telling you about the one? And the hair? And the walk?

MICHAEL: Red hair? Frizzled out? I saw her crossing the street near the bank when I was driving my mother today.

PEGGY: The most ridiculous thing that ever hit this town – isn't she, love?

MICHAEL: I was wondering who she was. She's a fine-looking bird.

JUNIOR (*his appreciation again for large ladies*): She's big.

PEGGY: Excuse me –

JUNIOR: No bother there, sham.

MICHAEL: No! Anne! Hope!

TOM: God!

PEGGY: Excuse me. That girl (*Josephine*) is a fine looking!

MICHAEL: Hmm?

PEGGY: I'm disappointed in you, Michael.

LIAM: Dirty aul' thing.

JUNIOR: I hear she fancies you, cowboy.

PEGGY (*at MICHAEL*): Tck!

MICHAEL: What?

PEGGY: Your taste. That girl.

MICHAEL: I'm not interested in her.

TOM: Gee, tough luck on Josephine.

PEGGY (*neurotically*): She's a disgusting girl, she's stupid – Did you see her neck?

MICHAEL: I only said –

PEGGY: Of course you didn't. Everyone is talking about her, she won't last long here. She wouldn't even be kept in this place only for it's up to its eyes in debt.

TOM: What's up with yeh?

PEGGY: Every man in the town, married and single, around her, like – like terriers.

TOM: What's up with yeh?

PEGGY: Ary I get sick of this marvellous stuff. Everything is 'marvellous' with Ridge.

MICHAEL: I only said –

PEGGY: Everything is 'marvellous' –

MICHAEL: Alright she isn't marvellous –

PEGGY: Everything is 'marvellous' –

TOM: What are ye – what's –

MICHAEL: But she's good-looking, good legs –

PEGGY: Everything is 'marvellous' –

JUNIOR: Jugs (*tits*) –

MICHAEL: She has a good job –

JUNIOR: Bottom –

PEGGY: Will she keep it – Will she keep it?

MICHAEL: Sexy-looking –

PEGGY: I don't agree, I don't agree! –

TOM: Wait a minute –

PEGGY: I don't agree! –

TOM: Hold on a minute –

PEGGY: Why should I agree? –

TOM: What are ye talking about! –

LIAM: She's a dirty aul' thing!

TOM (*silencing them*): What-are-ye-on-about! (*To* PEGGY:) What are you squealin' about?

PEGGY (*laughs suddenly, shrilly*): Ary shut up the lot of ye!

TOM: Are you finished? She's ridiculous alright.

PEGGY: Of course, she is –

TOM: And you're worse! The whole town is filled with – pookies.

LIAM: Strangers comin' in to run the town, fellas.

TOM (*groans to himself; then*): Anne! Annette! Missus! Where are they? Pint, gin, tonic, Scotch, two Irish! (*He feels* MICHAEL's *eyes on him:*) Yeh?

MICHAEL: Why don't you leave?

TOM: But I might lose my religion.

PEGGY: What's he (*Michael*) saying?

MICHAEL: You can still get out.

TOM: But what of my unfinished work here? My feverish social writings. Whose red pen would in merit and logic stand up to the passionate lucidity of Fr. O'Mara's sermons? Would you take my place, take me from my great vocation, and send me off to be setting myself on fire in the great adventure of the New World?

MICHAEL: There's still time.

PEGGY: What's he saying?

TOM: I've always taken my responsibilities seriously.

PEGGY: Of course you have, love.

TOM *is rolling his head in reaction to her.*

MICHAEL: What responsibilities for Christ's –

TOM: My mother, Jack, for Christ's sake, and my father, Jack, for Christ's sake. You enquired about my mother's health earlier but, for some strange reason or other, not my father's. Well, I can assure you they're both still alive. (*To* LIAM:) Don't be making wild-life faces at me, cowboy, I've got the goods on you.

LIAM: Didn't say a thing, fella.

Off, the town clock chiming ten.

MICHAEL: Do you know what he said about you one evening?

TOM: Who? (*Closes his eyes tightly; he doesn't want to know.*) Oh yes, our president.

MICHAEL: That if you didn't break out of it, none of us would.

TOM (*continues with eyes shut*): Break out of what?

MICHAEL: This.

TOM: Are you speaking geographically.

MICHAEL: Not necessarily. This talk all evening, and what it seems to represent?

TOM: What does it represent?

MICHAEL: You'd think the sixties never happened.

TOM: What did the sixties represent?

MICHAEL: Not this.

TOM: You-haven't-answered-a-single-question-all-night. You. too, are a great dealer in the abstract.

MICHAEL: The social movements of the minority's groups in the sixties, in towns, villages and cities, was the rising culture.

TOM: And *is* this the *rising* culture, begod!

ANNE *arrives with a tray of drinks.*

ANNE: Scotch, Michael? –

TOM: Ah, God bless yeh, Anne – Because despite the current swing to the right of the majorities, and the crusades of the christian fundamentalist majorities, promoting medieval notions of morality and reality, begod –

JUNIOR } Thanks, girl –
TOM } We the creative minorities are still here, begod, thank God, swinging to the left while they're swinging to the right. But we, the swinging-to-the-lefters will see those swinging-to-the-righters go swinging to their decline and disintegration. For! – And! – As you say! – even though we are the minority, it is always out of the creative cultural minority, it is always out of the creative cultural minority *groups* that change irrevocable comes about! Begod! What do you think of that? (*To* MICHAEL:) Happy? He's not happy still – begod! And why would he? I left out the big one. (*he is searching his pockets for money for the round.*)

LIAM: Good luck, fellas.

TOM: Because – fellas! – despite us, the representatives of the rising cultural minorities aforementioned, what is going on now, this minute, ablow in Paddy Joe Daly's? 'Put th' fuckin' blanket on the ground.' (*They laugh.*) But Paddy Joe Daly is not the enemy. He may personify it, the bullets in his bandy legs may symbolise it, the antics of his lump of a wife may dramatise it. But no – No! – the real enemy – the big one! – that we shall overcome, is the country-and-western system itself. Unyielding, uncompromising, in its drive for total sentimentality. A sentimentality I say that would have us all an unholy herd of Sierra Sues, sad-eyed inquisitors, sentimental Nazis, fascists, sectarianists, black-and-blue shirted nationalists, with spurs a-jinglin', all ridin' down the trail to Oranmore. Aw great, I knew I'd make ye all happy.

They laugh.

JUNIOR: Aw, Jasus, the twins. (*He slips the money for the round to* ANNE.)

MICHAEL: Do you ever go for rambles down to Woodlawn like we used to, Anne?

ANNE: Sometimes.

And she moves off to answer a tapping on the counter in the public bar – a toss of her head and a smile back at MICHAEL.

JUNIOR: The two of ye together might make up one decent man.

TOM: Well, whatever about me, I don't know what reason you had to hang around here, Sonny.

JUNIOR: We've had the complimenting stage, let that be an end to the insulting stage, and we'll get on to the singing stage. (*Singing:*) 'All in the April evening' –

TOM: And your father won't leave you the garage. One of the young brothers will have that.

JUNIOR (*smile disappears*): They can have it so they can.

TOM: They will.

LIAM: And that's the belief in the town.

JUNIOR (*back in form*): No! No! They're all off, the whole seven of them, to join the Palestine Police Force next week. Wuw! Jasus, Jasus . . . ! Come on, Peggy, you're the singer here. 'All in the –

PEGGY: Oh stop, Junior.

JUNIOR: Come on, that one, JJ's song –

PEGGY: I don't know when I sang last.

JUNIOR: 'All in the April evening, April airs –'

PEGGY: Stop, Junie. No. No –

JUNIOR } 'The sheep with their little lambs –' Come on!
PEGGY } No, no, no, no, no –
JUNIOR } Come on, come on –
PEGGY } No, no, no, no, no –

LIAM (*about to sing*): Fellas!

But PEGGY *is standing up; she sings the first line of 'All in the April evening'; then giggling; then fixing herself into the pose of the amateur contralto at the wedding, and singing deliberately off key and 'poshly' distorting the words.*

PEGGY: 'All in the April evening' – No, wait a minute . . . 'This is my lovely dee. This is thee dee I shall remember the dee' – Christina Jordan, did you ever hear her? – 'I'll remember, I'll remember – !' The cheek of her, not a note right in her head – 'I'll remember,

I'll remember – ' Jeeney! The eejit.
(*And she sits abruptly, hands over her mouth, giggling.*)

Tom exits to the Gents.

LIAM: Fellas! (*Fancies himself as a cowboy singer.*) 'There's a bridle hanging on the wall/There's a saddle in a lonely stall/You ask me why my tear drops fall/It's that bridle hanging on the wall/And that pony for my guide I used to ride down the trail watching the moon beam low-ow – ' (*The others stifling their laughter at him.*)

MICHAEL *and* JUNIOR *speaking simultaneously.*

MICHAEL: I need a drop more water for this one.

JUNIOR: One voice!

MICHAEL *joins* ANNE *at the bar.*

LIAM: 'And the pony for my guide I used to ride down the trail/he's gone where the good ponies go-ho/There's a bridle hanging on the wall . . . (*etc*)'

JUNIOR: Lovely hurlin', cowboy!

PEGGY: Smashin', Liam!

LIAM: I must mosey to the john again, fellas. Watch that latchyco, Anne! 'You ask me why my tear drops fall – '

TOM *entering as* LIAM *exits.*

TOM: Hey! And *your* sisters or young brother will have the farm.

LIAM: Sure, fella. (*Exits; returns a moment later in response to* TOM'*s* 'Hey!'.)

TOM: Hey! This eejit, this bollocks, with his auctioneering and tax-collecting and travel-agenting and property dealing and general greedy unprincipled poncing, and Sunday night dancing – Mr successfull-swinging-Ireland-In-The-Seventies! – and he's still – Jesus! – still – Jesus! – watching the few acres of bog at home, still – Jesus! – caught up in the few acres of bog around the house at home.

LIAM: What – what would you say, fella, if I said it was mine already?

TOM: I'd say, fella, that you're a liar.

LIAM: Well, it is mine.

TOM: As the bishop said to the actress.

LIAM: By deed – By deed! – The deeds are signed over to me.

PEGGY: But why suddenly all this talk tonight?

LIAM: And my young brother is studying to be a doctor.

TOM: Weren't *you* studying to be a doctor?

LIAM: Oh, d'yeh hear him now?

TOM: And quietly, it was a fortuitous outcome for the sick and the ailing that you never made it.

LIAM: D'yeh hear him now – Tro'sky!

TOM: And even if the young brother proves less thick than you, haven't the two spinster sisters a claim on the place?

LIAM: By deed.

PEGGY: But why –

TOM: No – No deed. Because your attempts, and the details of your attempts, and the details of the failure of your attempts to unseat them and evict them off the nine-and-a-half acre O'Brady estate are widely discussed and reported upon – in this town.

LIAM: I'm setting up my sisters in an antique shop.

JUNIOR (*quietly*): That's the place for them.

TOM: And quietly, and with little or no respect, I don't think either of them, in their advanced post-state of nubility, has much prospects of the bed.

LIAM: Oh d'yeh hear – I take exception to that remark.

TOM: Take what you like. Give us a drop of water here too for this one, Anne. So, the next time you see someone driving around in a Merc just think of him.

ANNE *arrives to add water to* TOM'*s drink.*

LIAM: Why don't you get married?

TOM: Why don't yeh yourself? (*To* ANNE:) That's fine. (*He is rooting in his pockets again for further coins to pay for the last round.*)

LIAM: Afraid of his Mammy and Daddy.

And, d'ye know, he has to hand over his paypacket to his Mammy intact, every week, into her hand.

TOM: I get paid by cheque, Liam – monthly. (*To* ANNE:) Just a sec.

ANNE: Its paid for –

TOM: Just a sec –

LIAM: Then cheque, countersigned, it has to be handed over to Mammy.

PEGGY: Aa, change the subject, lads.

ANNE: Junie paid for it.

JUNIOR: Sure poor auld Liam couldn't go bringing a woman into a house where there's three of them already –

PEGGY (*offering* TOM *two pounds*): Here, love –

TOM (*to* ANNE): What?

JUNIOR: Jasus, they'd ate each other.

TOM (*to* LIAM): You are the worst of the worst type of a ponce of a modern fuckin' gombeen man, that's all that's to be said about it.

ANNE: It's paid for, Tom.

LIAM: There's an answer for that one too.

TOM: Yes, Liam.

JUNIOR: It's paid for, it's okay –

LIAM (*only just containing his drunken fury*): My birthright!

TOM (*to* JUNIOR): What?
PEGGY Here, loveen –
TOM (*to* PEGGY): What?
LIAM That's no argument!
TOM (*to* LIAM): What?
JUNIOR It's okay, it's paid for –

TOM: What?

LIAM: The eldest son, fella!

TOM (*to* LIAM): What are you talking about? (*to* ANNE:) And who asked anyone to pay for it! (*To himself.*) Tck! – Look – Jesus – (*To* LIAM:) Look, don't talk to me about argument – Look – lookit, don't talk to me at all! (*To* PEGGY:) Will-you-put-that (*money*) – away! (*To* LIAM:) You're only a fuckin' bunch of keys! (*To* ANNE:) Bring us another round!

ANNE *returns to bar.*

PEGGY: Why don't you drive up and bring Gloria down. Do, Junie.

JUNIOR: Oh-oh.

PEGGY: Aa go on, good lad, do, do.

JUNIOR: Won't I be seeing her later!

LIAM (*quietly*): I'll squeeze your head for you some night, Ryan.

TOM: Good man, My round is coming, is it Anne?

LIAM: Cause I hate ye all – and all belongin' to ye!

He sweeps up his newspaper, then wrong-foots himself in his indecision as to whether to leave or not, remembers he has a stake in the place and exits to the Gents.

JUNIOR: Once you go once you're knackered for the evening.

MICHAEL *laughing with* JUNIOR, *then* TOM *starts to chuckle and he joins* MICHAEL *and* ANNE *at the counter.*

ANNE: But he's a lovely dancer though.

TOM, MICHAEL, JUNIOR *laughing again.* ANNE *joining in.*

TOM: Now: the new generation: 'you ask me why my tear drops fall, it's that pony hangin' on the wall'.

Excepting PEGGY *they are laughing again. And* JUNIOR *is now rising to go to the Gents.*

JUNIOR: Jasus, Jasus – (*To* PEGGY:) Excuse me, the call of the wild, the enemy within – you have a great pair of kidneys, Ridge! shake hand with the devil, wuw!

And he has exited to the Gents. PEGGY *now continues self-consciously isolated at the table, her back to the others. And they have all but forgotten her.* TOM's *mood is now pacificatory.*

ANNE: What part are you in, Michael?

MICHAEL: Well, I'm not working, obviously, at the moment, but –

TOM: What part of America she's asking, eejit.

MICHAEL *looks at him:* TOM *gestures/shrugs that no malice is intended.*

MICHAEL: New York.

ANNE: What's it like?

MICHAEL: Well, it's not too bad at all. Were you ever in the States?

ANNE: No, but I was in London last summer. Two of us went over and we stayed with some friends of daddy's.

MICHAEL: Did you? Did he arrange it for you?

ANNE: Yes.

PEGGY (*isolated*): Indeed I was there myself for a few months once.

Nobody is listening to her.

ANNE: We went to a place – I said I was eighteen – and got a job in an ice-cream factory.

PEGGY: I was putting the tops on polish tins.

ANNE *has set up the other round.*

TOM: Make that a double for your man (*Michael*) and mine the same and tell your mother to put it on the slate.

MICHAEL: I'll get it.

TOM: Don't be so extravagant with your mother's money. (*Then gestures/shrugs again to Michael's reaction: no malice intended; and showing Michael the few coins in his hand:*) Look at the way I am myself.

ANNE: And will I make the others doubles?

TOM: Are yeh coddin' me!

MICHAEL: What would you say to a stroll down to Woodlawn tomorrow, Anne?

She nods. This forthright reply, the immediate success of his proposition surprises and stops him for a moment.

ANNE: Fine.

MICHAEL: What?

ANNE: That'd be lovely . . . what time?

He gestures: what time would suit her. Four?

MICHAEL (*nods*): . . . Where shall I . . .? (*meet you*)

ANNE: The Bridge.

MICHAEL: Ah! The Bridge.

LIAM *comes in and stands away from them, aloof, sulking.* MICHAEL *has started singing/performing – perhaps Rex Harrison/James Cagney style – for* ANNE.

MICHAEL: 'At seventeen he falls in love quite madly with eyes of tender blue.'

TOM (*to* LIAM): There's a drink there for you, bollocks.

MICHAEL: 'At twenty-four, he gets it rather badly with eyes of different hue.'

TOM (*to* ANNE): Give him (*Liam*) that.

MICHAEL: 'At thirty-five, you'll find him flirting sadly with two, or three, or more.'

TOM (*edging him further away from the others*): Come over here a minute.

MICHAEL: 'When he fancies he is past love' –

TOM: This is nonsense, this caper all evening.

MICHAEL: 'It is then he meets his last love –'

TOM: Don't mind that. Hmm?

MICHAEL: Well, what's up with you?

TOM: Nothing. What's up with you?

MICHAEL: Not a thing.

TOM: Well then. Good luck!

MICHAEL: Good luck!

They toast each other. Short pause. Both looking down; can't think of anything to say.

MICHAEL: 'And he loves her as he's never loved before.'

TOM: I can't help it . . . I can't feel anything about anything anymore.

MICHAEL: I know.

TOM: What?

MICHAEL: I know what you mean.

TOM: You're the only friend I have . . . Wha'?

MICHAEL: Mutual.

TOM: Say something.

MICHAEL (*quietly*): Yahoo?

TOM: Did JJ admire me?

MICHAEL: Yeh.

TOM (*to himself*): But what good is that? I don't think he understood my (*sigh*) situation. Isn't that what people want? What? A true and honest account of the situation first. What? A bit of clarity and sanity. Definition. Facts. Wha'? . . . Did he admire me?

MICHAEL: Yeh.

TOM: More than the others, you said.

MICHAEL: Bigger expectations (*shrugs*) – I suppose.

TOM: What? . . . Will I tell you something: What? Will I? Will I tell you something confidential? What? will I? I never lost an argument in my life. What? What d'yeh think of that? What? Isn't that something? . . . But you're doing well.

MICHAEL: No.

TOM: No! You are!

MICHAEL: Setting myself on fire.

TOM: You're doing well, you're doing well, someone has to be doing well, and we're all delighted, we are, we are, we really are . . . The only friend I have, bollocks, with your cigarette holder in your top pocket. (MICHAEL's *hand guiltily to his top* pocket. TOM *intensely, drunkenly.*) Why didn't yeh use it, why didn't yeh use it?

MICHAEL: Just one of them filter things.

TOM: But why didn't yeh use it? D'yeh see what I mean? . . . (*Genuinely pained.*) I try. I can't help it.

PEGGY (*rising, approaching, smiling bravely*): What are the men talking about? I know well: the women are always left out of the juicy things.

TOM (*frowning to himself*): What?

PEGGY: Cheers!

TOM: What?

MICHAEL: Cheers, Peggy.

PEGGY: Do you ever meet anyone from round here over there, Michael?

MICHAEL: Oh, I met Casey.

PEGGY: Aa did yeh. Joe? D'yeh hear that, love. How's he getting on?

MICHAEL: Fine. Getting the dollars regular every week, hot and cold water in his room, and paying no income tax.

PEGGY: Indeed we heard the opposite.

TOM: Hold it a second, Peg –

PEGGY: Someone who saw him over there –

TOM: A minute, Peg –

PEGGY: No shirt, an old pullover, no heels to his shoes–

TOM: Why do you always reduce everything!

PEGGY: . . . Well it was you told me.

Off, the town clock ringing eleven.

MICHAEL: One for the road, Anne. (*Extricating himself from* TOM *and* PEGGY.)

JUNIOR (*off, and entering*): 'Oi, oi, oi, Delilah, phy, phy, phy, Delilah –' (*He surveys the room.*) Jasus, I was at better parties in the Mercy Convent!

MICHAEL (*kicking cigarette holder across the room*): I don't give a damn! A walk in the woods, a breath of fresh air, right Anne!

She smiles, nods.

JUNIOR: Into the net, Seaneen!

LIAM (*glowering; a warning*): Watch it. (*The cigarette holder flying past him.*)

JUNIOR: Keep the faith, cowboy! I'll sing a hymn to Mary, he says, the mother of them all!

MICHAEL: No! Nice and quiet, Junie. (*Sings:*) 'I'll sing a hymn to Mary.'

JUNIOR ⎫ 'The mother of my God'
MICHAEL ⎭ 'The mother of my God, the virgin of all virgins'

LIAM (ANNE *has brought a drink to* him): Nothing for me. (*He spills the drink* TOM *bought him and the one that has just arrived on the floor and continues brooding.*)

JUNIOR (*singing*): 'The virgin of all virgins of God's own dearly son!'

MICHAEL ⎫ 'Of David's royal blood'.
JUNIOR ⎭ 'Of David's royal blood'.

MICHAEL: Nice and quiet, Junie. (*They*

sing together, ANNE *singing with them:*) 'Oh teach me Holy Mary a loving song to frame/When wicked men blaspheme Thee/I'll love and bless Thy name/Oh Lily of the Valley . . .' (*Etc., until it is stopped by Tom's attack on Peggy.*)

TOM (*through the above, muttering*): Ugliness, ugliness, ugliness. (*He becomes aware of* PEGGY.) What are you looking at?

PEGGY *has been casting hopeful glances at him. She does not reply.* MICHAEL, JUNIOR *and* ANNE *continue softly – under the following:*

TOM (*to* PEGGY): Do even *you* admire me? My feverish social writings.

PEGGY: It's late, love.

TOM: My generous warm humour.

PEGGY: I'd like to go home, love.

TOM: What?

PEGGY: I don't feel well, love.

TOM: What? Well, go! Who's stopping yeh? My God, you walk up and down from your own house twenty times a day with your short little legs! No one will molest you! We're all mice!

She hurries from the room, stops in the front doorway, can't leave, her life invested in TOM *– and hangs in the doorway crying. Off, the church clock ringing eleven.*

MICHAEL (*about to follow* PEGGY): Ah Jesus, sham.

TOM (*stops him with his voice*): Hey! (*Then:*) Ugliness, ugliness, ugliness!

ANNE: She's not feeling well.

TOM (*stopping* MICHAEL *again with his voice and warning him not to interfere*): Hey! Gentlemen! Jim! My extravagant adventurous spirit. And the warm wild humour of Liam over there. And all those men of prudence and endeavour who would sell the little we have left of charm, character, kindness and madness to any old bidder with a pound, a dollar, a mark or a yen. And all those honest and honourable men who campaign for the right party and collect taxes on the chapel road. And all those honest and honourable men who are cutting down the trees for

making – Easter-egg boxes!

MICHAEL: That's more like it!

TOM: Is it? (*Stopping* MICHAEL *again from going out to* PEGGY.) Hey!

JUNIOR (*quietly to* MICHAEL): Leave it so.

MICHAEL: Let us remember that civility is not a sign of weakness –

TOM (*mimics Kennedy*): 'And that sincerity is always subject to proof.' You all love speeches, rhetoric, crap, speeches. Right! 'I know you all, and will a while uphold the unyoked humour of your idleness.' I was always a better actor than you, better at everything than anyone round here. 'Yet herein will I imitate the sun who doth permit the base contagious clouds to smother up his beauty from the world!'

MICHAEL: 'But when he please again to be himself – '

TOM: *That! 'That* when he please again to be himself, being wanted, he may be more wondered at, by breaking through the foul and ugly mists of vapour that seem to strangle him,' tangle him, bangle him . . .

VOICE (*off*): Goodnight to ye now.

JUNIOR: Good luck, Johnny!

ANNE: Good night, Johnny!

MICHAEL: Deoch an dorais, Tom, come on.

TOM (*quietly: going – now docilely – to bar with* MICHAEL): 'And when this loose behaviour I throw off, by how much better than my word I am, my reformation glittering o'er my faults shall show more goodly and attract more eyes than this which hath no foil to set it off.'

Through this last section, PEGGY *is in the doorway – she has had her head to the wall, crying – now listening, hoping someone will come out to her. She starts to sing – at first tentatively, like someone making noises to attract attention to herself. Then progressively, going into herself, singing essentially for herself: quietly, looking out at the night, her back to us, the sound representing*

*her loneliness, the gentle desperation of
her situation, and the memory of a
decade ago. Her song creates a stillness
over them all.*

PEGGY: 'All in the April evening, April
airs were abroad/ The sheep with their
little lambs passed me by on the road/
The sheep with their little lambs passed
me by on the road/ All in the April
evening I thought on the lamb of God.'

At the conclusion of the song, MISSUS
coming down the stairs. PEGGY
*instinctively moving out of the doorway
to stand outside the pub.*

TOM *(quietly)*: 'I'll so offend to make
offence a skill, redeeming time when
men think least I will.'

MISSUS *comes in to collect a broom.*

MISSUS: Come on now, boys, it's gone
the time.

TOM: One for the road, Missus.

MISSUS *(returning to the public bar)*:
And Johnny Quinn is half-way home
the back way to his bed by now.

JUNIOR: Well, that's it.

LIAM: Well, that's not it! *(He rattles a
chair: his statement of challenge to
fight.)* I can quote more Shakespeare
than any man here! *(He glances at each
of them in turn, culminating with
TOM.)*

MISSUS *(off)*: Drink up now, boys!

LIAM: 'And still they marvelled and the
wonder grew, that one *big* head could
carry all he knew.'

TOM *(eyes closed)*: Shakespeare?

LIAM: No. Goldsmith.

JUNIOR: Well said, boy.

LIAM: *The Deserted Village,* fella.

MISSUS *(off)*: Finish up now, boys!

LIAM: Ryan! The village schoolmaster
. . . The f-f-f- . . . The f-f-f . . . Ryan!
*(LIAM breathing heavily through his
nose, jaws set, fists clenched.* TOM, *still
with eyes closed, arms limply at his
sides, turns to* LIAM, *nods, prepared to
be hit, perhaps wanting to be hit.)* The
village schoolmaster.

TOM *eyes closed, nods again.* LIAM

*unsure as to whether or not he is being
mocked, glancing at the others . . . then
suddenly grabs Tom's hand and shakes
it.*

MISSUS *(coming in with broom which
she gives to* ANNE*)*: And the guards
are on the prowl these nights.

TOM *(to* LIAM*)*: So are we quits?

LIAM: Okay, fella.

TOM *(glancing at* MICHAEL*)*: But
we're not quite through.

PEGGY *comes in timidly, gets her coat,
hopeful glances at Tom.*

They all speak at once:

MICHAEL: We're going to start again
with a constant flow of good ideas. 'Let
the word go forth . . .'

TOM *(by way of apology to* PEGGY*)*:
Just . . . just a bit of Shakespeare.

MICHAEL: 'From this time and place,
to friend and foe alike, that the torch
has been passed to a new generation.'

MISSUS: Come on now boys, come on.

JUNIOR: Well I must be getting home
anyway to Gloria – Oosh!

Until:

MICHAEL: 'Let every nation know,
whether it wishes us good or ill, that
we shalll pay any price, bear any
burden, endure any hardship, to ensure
the success and the survival of liberty.'

MISSUS *(to* LIAM*)*: Call again during
the week, Liam – why wouldn't yeh –
and have a nice bite of tea with us.
And thanks, the good boy, Liam,
Drink up now, boys, and haven't ye all
night tomorrow night, and thanks,
thank ye all now. Yas. And safe home.
D'ye know now.

*She has switched off the lights in the
lounge – (the spill of light from the
hallway and from the public bar now
lights the lounge) – and she is on her
way along the hallway, upstairs,
counting the money from her cardigan
pockets.* ANNE *is about to exit with the
broom and some dirty glasses to public
bar.*

MICHAEL: Goodnight, princess, till it
be morrow.

ANNE: Goodnight. (*And exits to public bar.*)

They are pulling on their coats, etc. in silence. JUNIOR scrutinising the table for any drink that might have been left unfinished.

MICHAEL: But it wasn't a bad night.

JUNIOR: It wasn't a bad auld night alright. (*And eager for further confirmation of this*:) Wha'?

LIAM (*muttering*): I wouldn't advise anyone to go messing with my plans.

MICHAEL: And I'll be wheeling Annette tomorrow.

TOM: Good man.

PEGGY: Oh come on, loveen, I'm perished.

LIAM (*muttering*): I know a thing or two about you, Ridge.

PEGGY: What's he muttering about?

MICHAEL (*singing quietly*): 'Sure no letter I'll be mailin'' –

LIAM: It's not right.

MICHAEL: 'For soon will I be sailin'' –

PEGGY: Brrah, come on, loveen.

TOM (*sudden thought*): Wait a minute.

MICHAEL: 'And I'll bless the ship that takes me – '

TOM: It's not right alright –

MICHAEL: 'To my dear auld Erin's shore – '

TOM: Michael. Anne.

MICHAEL } 'There I'll settle down forever – '

TOM { Serious – Michael – Don't start messin'.

MICHAEL } What?

LIAM: Don't start messin' fella. Invested time and money. My – our territory. Right, Tom? Junie?

MICHAEL (*laughs*): 'There's a pretty spot in Ireland – '

TOM: Michael. Are you listening?

MICHAEL: It's not a jiggy-jig job. JJ's daughter. A walk in the wood, a breath of fresh air. (*He looks at their serious faces.*) What? You know it's

nothing else.

TOM: We don't.

LIAM: We don't, fella. A word to Mrs Kilkelly – or to Anne herself.

TOM: So cop on.

MICHAEL: Who?

TOM: You.

LIAM: You, fella. Don't infringe.

MICHAEL looks incredulously at TOM.

TOM (*shrugs/blandly*): Liam's territory. Right Liam, you nearly have it sold, right? Good. Even if they don't know it. Better for Missus, Anne. Better for – Put a bomb under it if you like. Better for everyone. Reality. So that's okay. And we'll fix you up with the gammy one tomorrow. Josephine. Right, Junie?

JUNIOR (*has enough of them*): I'm off. Jasus, I only meant to have the two pints. (*To MICHAEL:*) D'yeh want a lift? (*To TOM and PEGGY:*) D'ye want a lift? Okay, see ye.

He goes off, puffing a tuneless whistle and a few moments later we hear him drive away.

PEGGY: Oh come on, loveen, your mother will have your life.

TOM: Don't be silly!

LIAM: So that's okay then, Tom?

TOM (*quietly but firmly*): Yeh.

LIAM: Okay, fellas, God bless.

He exits.

TOM: . . . I hope he remembers he has no clutch in his car or he'll be all night looking for it.

LIAM'*s car starting up and driving away.*

Come on, we'll walk you home.

MICHAEL: I'm dead sober. And I'm certainly not as confused as I was.

TOM (*pacificatory*): Ary! You're only an eejit, Ridge.

MICHAEL *nods.*

PEGGY: Y'are.

MICHAEL *nods.*

TOM (*mock gruffness*): Y'are!

MICHAEL: But I know what I came home for.

TOM: Come on, we'll walk yeh down.

MICHAEL: No, I'm – okay.

TOM: Give us a shout tomorrow.

PEGGY: Night-night, Michael.

TOM: We didn't get a chance to have a right talk.

PEGGY: God bless, take care.

TOM: Good luck, sham.

MICHAEL: Good luck.

TOM *and* PEGGY *exit.*

TOM (*off*): Give us a shout tomorrow!

PEGGY (*off*): 'Bye-'bye, Michael!

TOM (*off*): Will yeh?

PEGGY (*off*): 'Bye-'bye, Michael!

TOM (*off*): Will yeh?

PEGGY (*off*): 'Bye-'bye!

MICHAEL *continues standing there. He looks up and around at the room. He finishes his drink and is about to leave.*

MISSUS (*off*): Leave the light on in the hall, Annette, in case.

The light is switched off in the public bar and ANNE *enters and discovers* MICHAEL. *Her simple grave expression.*

MICHAEL (*whispers*): I have to go in the morning.

ANNE (*silently*): What?

MICHAEL: Have to go in the morning. (*He smiles, shrugs.*) They've probably cut down the rest of the wood by now, anyway.

ANNE: There's still the stream.

MICHAEL: Yeh. But I have to go. Tell JJ I'm sorry I didn't see him. Tell him . . . (*He wants to add something but cannot find the words yet.*) . . . Tell him I love him.

She nods, she smiles, she knows. He waits for another moment to admire her, then he walks off. ANNE *continues in the window as at the*

beginning of the play, smiling her gentle hope out at the night.